PLANTATION
Aspects of seventeenth-century
Ulster society

PLANTATION

Aspects of seventeenth-century
Ulster society

edited by
Brendan Scott and John Dooher

ULSTER HISTORICAL FOUNDATION
ULSTER LOCAL HISTORY TRUST

First published 2013
by Ulster Historical Foundation
49 Malone Road, Belfast BT9 6RY
www.ancestryireland.com
www.booksireland.org.uk

Ulster Local History Trust
18 Clonaog Valley, Lisnaskea
Co. Fermanagh, BT92 0JL
www.ulht.org.uk

© ULHT/UHF and the authors
ISBN: 978-1-909556-09-6

Printed by Bell & Bain Ltd.
Cover Design by Dunbar Design
Typesetting by FPM Publishing

Contents

Abbreviations and Conventions

Armagh Pub. Lib.	Armagh Public Library
BL	British Library, London
Bod. Lib.	Bodleian Library, Oxford
Cal. S.P. Ire.	*Calendar of state papers relating to Ireland* (London, 1874–)
CJ	*Journals of the House of Commons*
CSPD	*Calendar of state papers domestic* (London, 1872–1903)
CSPV	*Calendar of state papers and manuscripts, relating to English affairs, existing in the archives and collections of Venice, and in other libraries of Northern Italy* (London, 1864-1927)
HMC	Historical Manuscripts Commission (London, 1874–)
LJ	*Journals of the House of Lords*
OED	*Oxford English Dictionary*
ODNB	*Oxford Dictionary of National Biography*
PRONI	Public Records Office Northern Ireland, Belfast
QUB	Queen's University, Belfast
TCD	Trinity College Dublin
TNA	The National Archives, London

The year is taken to begin on 1 January, and not, as was the custom in the seventeenth century, 25 March.

Contributors

JOHN B. CUNNINGHAM was born in Ballyshannon, County Donegal, but has lived all of his life in Fermanagh. He was headmaster of St Davog's P.S. from 1969 to 1996 and took early retirement to write and become a tour guide. His writing includes about forty published works and about 150 published articles in various journals, dealing mostly with local history and similar themes. He is chairman of Fermanagh Authors' Association and Erne Heritage Tour Guides and a member of a number of other organisations related to tourism and local history.

PATRICK FITZGERALD (Ph.D.) completed his Queen's University Belfast thesis on the subject of 'Poverty and Vagrancy in Early Modern Ireland' in 1994. Following a period working as Curator of Emigration History at the Ulster-American Folk Park, Omagh, he took up his current post as Lecturer and Development Officer with the Mellon Centre for Migration Studies at the Ulster-American Folk Park in 1998. Since 1996, he has been teaching at postgraduate level with Queen's University Belfast. He has published numerous articles and papers related to Irish migration history and is the co-author, with Brian Lambkin, of *Migration in Irish History, 1607–2007* (2008).

RAYMOND GILLESPIE (Ph.D.) is a professor of history at NUI Maynooth. He has written widely on the economic and social history of early modern Ireland and in particular the transformation of the province of Ulster in the seventeenth century.

ELAINE MURPHY (Ph.D.) is a lecturer in maritime/naval history at Plymouth University. She was previously research associate at the University of Cambridge on a project to prepare a new critical edition of the writings and speeches of Oliver Cromwell. From 2007–2010, Elaine was an associate editor on the 1641 Depositions Project, based in Trinity College Dublin. Her book, *Ireland and the War at Sea, 1641–1660*, was published by the Royal Historical Society in 2012.

ANDREW ROBINSON (Ph.D.) was formerly a research assistant for the Institute of Ulster Scots Studies. He has recently completed a thesis at the University of Ulster entitled, '"Not otherwise worthy to be named, but as a firebrand brought from Ireland to inflame this Kingdom": The political and cultural milieu of Sir John Clotworthy during the Stuart Civil Wars'. He has worked on the Wars of the Three Kingdoms in County Monaghan and and the 1641 rising in Clogher. His main areas of research interest include the plantation of Ulster, early modern Protestant identity, biblical rhetoric and deuteronomic history during the Stuart Civil Wars.

WILLIAM ROULSTON (Ph.D.) is Research Director of the Ulster Historical Foundation. He has written and edited a number of books, including *Researching Scots-Irish Ancestors* (2005), *Restoration Strabane, 1660–1714: economy and society in provincial Ireland* (2007), and *Three centuries of life in a Tyrone parish: a history of Donagheady from 1600 to 1900* (2010).

BRENDAN SCOTT (Ph.D.) has written and edited a number of books and articles on religion and society in early modern Ireland, including *Religion and reformation in the Tudor diocese of Meath* (2006), *Cavan 1609–53: plantation, war and religion* (2007) and most recently prepared for publication Robert Hunter's edition of *The Ulster Port Books, 1612–15* (2012). He has lectured at NUI Maynooth and was research officer at Cavan County Museum, 2006–09.

Foreword

The Ulster Local History Trust was set up in 1980 by the Federation for Ulster Local Studies to help raise standards in local history within the nine counties. By 1990, the Trust had secured enough capital to begin making small grants to further this work. Most of the grants were devoted to assist local history publishing, but other projects were considered and supported.

The Trust gave assistance to exhibitions, essay prizes, a sculpture project, video documentaries and oral history, as well as supporting over 100 publications. The titles here ranged from numerous local histories to works initiated by the Royal Irish Academy and the Institute of Irish Studies. The trustees are always keen to reward improved layouts and better design as well as the creation of indexes.

Since 2001, the Trust has organised a conference every two years. The six we have staged have sought to address important themes in local and national history. The first three examined the heritage of townlands, the significance of border landscapes and the concept of migration both today and in the past. The papers read at these conferences have been published and to date *The Debateable Land* (2002), *The Heart's Townland* (2004) and *Migration and Myth* (2006) have preserved the work and impact of these events.

The plantation of Ulster was such a defining event in the history of Ireland that the Trust held two conferences to look at its four hundredth anniversary. In 2008, we held a two-day conference in Monaghan to take a detailed look at the initial years of the plantation with the title 'Across the Narrow Sea; plantations in Ulster' while two years later in Armagh we examined the longer-term consequences of the event under the banner 'Plantation and Retribution: Ulster 1610–1641'.

This volume contains five of the papers given at the two conferences as well as two additional chapters on the 1641 period. It is the Trust's fourth conference proceedings and will I hope provide a valuable record of what were two highly successful events.

We are indebted to the Ulster Historical Foundation for their assistance in bringing this work into print. They have already an impressive record in history publishing and have recently produced four books that cover much of the unpublished research of R.J. Hunter, a recognised authority on the Ulster Plantation. The seventeenth-century material in this volume will we hope complement that research.

I would like to thank Ms Shirley Clerkin, the County Monaghan Heritage Officer, for her support in running the 2008 conference and Ms Laura Houghton of the R.J. Hunter Committee for providing funds to help with the 2010 event. The Trust is likewise grateful to two of our own trustees for the key roles taken by them in organising the two conferences – Mr Aidan Walsh in Monaghan and Dr Brendan Scott in Armagh. We are also indebted to Dr Scott who, along with another trustee Mr John Dooher, has edited the current volume.

JACK JOHNSTON
Chairman

Introduction

In this era of commemorations and re-evaluations, the Ulster Local History Trust has been very conscious of its mission to promote a deeper awareness and understanding of our troubled past. With this in mind, recent biannual conferences have sought to bring the fruits of new research and reinterpretations of our past to the attention of the wider public, not only in Ulster, but throughout Ireland.

A two-day conference in 2008 looked at the theme of plantation and migration in the seventeenth century under the title 'Across the narrow sea: plantations in Ulster'. At this conference, leading historians reviewed the historiography of the subject and examined the local, national and wider impact and consequences of the influx of new settlers to Ireland. Professors Patrick Duffy, Raymond Gillespie, Mary O'Dowd, James Stevens Curl and Dr Patrick Fitzgerald examined various aspects of the Ulster Plantation, while Johnny Cunningham, Dr William Roulston and Siobhan McDermott emphasised the lessons to be drawn from local in-depth studies.

This was followed in 2010 by a one-day conference under the title 'Plantation and Retribution: Ulster 1610–1641', with a range of talks assessing key issues during that period. Dr Brendan Scott and Dr William Roulston provided evaluations on the limitations of the success of the religious aspects of the plantation programme while Professor Jane Ohlmeyer, Dr David Edwards and Professor Aidan Clarke reviewed the pressures from above and below that culminated in the events of the 1641 rising. The final lecture of the programme was provided by Professor John Morrill in tribute to a leading scholar of the plantation period, Robert (Bob) Hunter.

A number of the papers from these conferences, along with others commissioned for this publication have been made available here and it is the hope of the editors that this collection of essays will further develop the process of investigation and understanding into these early decades of the seventeenth century, a period in our history which has continued to resonate so deeply over the centuries with deeply entrenched viewpoints, and which still provokes heated argument.

The Trust is deeply indebted to all those scholars who spoke at the above-mentioned conferences and who have contributed to this volume. It is hoped that the wide variety of topics and approaches will be of interest to many people and stimulate further investigation and research into this much studied period. Brendan Scott and I wish to acknowledge the support of our fellow trustees on the Ulster Local History Trust and Fintan Mullan and Dr William Roulston of the Ulster Historical Foundation for their commitment to this project. Finally the Trust gratefully acknowledges the support of the R.J. Hunter Committee in making this publication possible and hopes that it will help in some small measure to pay tribute to one of the recent pioneers of early seventeenth-century Irish history.

JOHN DOOHER

When the British came to Ulster: migration, memory and myth

Patrick Fitzgerald

The central preoccupation of this paper is with the chronology of migration from Britain to Ulster and the exploration of the proposition that, on the cusp of the four hundredth anniversary of the Jacobean Plantation of the six escheated Ulster counties, we still tend to take a rather narrow view of the peopling process which spanned, what Sam Hanna Bell dubbed, the Narrow Sea.[1] Working in the Mellon Centre for Migration Studies at the Ulster American Folk Park over the course of the last decade, I have been repeatedly struck by the regularity with which North American roots tourists in search of Ulster-Scots lineage misread the chronology of migration from Scotland to Ireland and indeed later migration from Ireland to North America.[2] Concerning ourselves primarily here with the former of these two migrations, I am often confronted by those whose migration timeline charts the movement from Scotland to Ireland as an essentially early Stuart phenomenon. Nor is this distorted impression of the sequencing of migration purely due to family lore as many popular historical accounts published on both sides of the Atlantic tend to perpetuate this version of the narrative. Reviewing some of these publications will form part of the substance of this paper.

Before proceeding too much further, however, it is probably worthwhile to draw something of a distinction between the domains of Academic and Public history. Whilst I do not expect the figures quoted below to surprise those academically engaged in the period, I would anticipate that the patterns of migration mapped out may jar with those more familiar with the 'received version' communicated at a more 'popular' level. If this thesis is accurate it may suggest that historians continue to face real challenges in transferring their research findings to the widest possible public audience.[3]

I would like to proceed by offering some personal reflections relating to the reading of the landscape in my own locale of south Tyrone. As an immigrant or 'blow-in' (in the vernacular) to the small mid-Tyrone village of Seskinore, I can recall my initial impression, when I arrived more than a decade ago, that this classic estate village, with Church of Ireland chapel of ease, estate-sponsored school and broad main street, likely had its origins in the Jacobean Plantation of Ulster. In fact, the extant evidence suggests that the village really only began to take shape in the 1780s, following the marriage of Mary Perry to Alexander McClintock from County Louth but of a family originally from Argyllshire. Although a British planter population was already established in the vicinity in the generation prior to 1641, the development of the estate and the attraction of migrants from Britain or elsewhere in Ulster owed most to the energies of the Perry family, who were granted fee farm lands here in 1662 by Sir Audley Mervyn (lawyer and politician, 1603–75). Although the surname Perry (or Porry) appears amongst the Planter tenantry as early as 1630, the James Perry who was granted lands in 1662 and established his initial seat at nearby Perrymount, was most likely a recent immigrant from Wales.[4]

Similarly, if we turn our attention to another slightly larger Tyrone estate village, Caledon, on the Armagh border, we detect a not dissimilar pattern of delayed development. In 1614, the lands here appear to have been given over, somewhat unusually, to a female Irish grantee, Catherine Ní Neill and only came into the possession of William Hamilton, whose family originated in Lanarkshire, but had been settled in north-west Tyrone for a generation, after the Cromwellian victory in 1649.

Even by 1666, only six British hearth owners were recorded here and again the development of the village only really began under Lord Orrery (John Boyle, 5th earl of Cork and 5th earl of Orrery, writer and friend of Jonathan Swift, 1707–62) in the late 1740s and then most significantly under the Alexanders (James Alexander, 1st earl of Caledon, 1730–1802, son of Nathaniel Alexander, alderman of Londonderry, returned to Ireland from India a very wealthy man in 1772) who acquired the estate in 1776.[5]

Although it does seem entirely appropriate in a publication sponsored by the Ulster Local History Trust to introduce these two localised examples, the primary purpose for doing so is to attempt to illustrate three wider points. Firstly, that the Ulster Plantation was explicitly a British and 'unionist' project. Arguably a central reason why James VI and I took such a direct personal interest in the scheme was because he recognised it as a vehicle which could give tangible expression to his desire (one might even suggest fixation) to promote a constitutional union between England and Scotland and to bolster a Stuart dynasty which could exercise effective governance across the three kingdoms.[6] Secondly, in order to highlight that migration from Britain to Ulster remained relatively modest during the first half of the seventeenth century and accelerated after 1650 towards a peak, of particularly Scottish immigration, during the final decade of the century.[7]

Thirdly, to illustrate the extent to which processes initiated in the 1610s often took significantly longer (several generations) to fulfil their potential.[8]

So let us return from these local examples to consider the historical narrative set out in the popular literature. A brief review of some of the works targeted primarily at a popular audience and published since the Millennium serves to illustrate the point alluded to in the introduction. In the year 2000 Ron Chepesiuk published a book entitled *The Scotch-Irish: From the North of Ireland to the Making of America* in North Carolina. The opening paragraph of the preface offers the following account:

> The Scotch-Irish were originally lowland Scots who migrated in considerable numbers to the province of Ulster in Ireland in the seventeenth century to participate in the colonial scheme established during the reign of James I (1603–25) and then in the next century, because of economic and religious reasons emigrated once more to America.[9]

Although to be fair to the author he later acknowledges in a sentence the migration of 'an estimated 50,000 Scots' in the years between 1690 and 1697, this sits against a full chapter of eighteen pages devoted to the Jacobean Plantation.[10] I would suggest that there is little here to dissuade the average reader from deducing that a trans-Atlantic emigrant ancestor of the early eighteenth century came from a family which had been in Ulster for three or four generations. Simultaneously on this side of the ocean, Billy Kennedy published *Heroes of the Scotch-Irish in America* which in two pages seeks to summarise Scottish Presbyterian settlement in Ulster. Again to be fair to the author, he states in the opening paragraph that 'movement continued throughout the seventeenth century in what was known as the Scottish Plantation'.[11] However, in the remainder of this summation, Kennedy only takes the story as far as 1642 and makes no explicit reference at all to migration during the second half of the century. In 2004, James Webb, elected as Democratic Senator for Virginia in 2006, authored a volume entitled *Born Fighting: How the Scots-Irish Shaped America* in which, during the course of a chapter dealing with the Ulster Plantation, he does make reference to the volume of migration which followed the early Stuart plantation. Yet, further on in the text, while discussing the origins of the Ulster emigrants who left for colonial America between 1715 and 1775, he claims 'many of these families had spent more than a hundred years in Ireland. Almost all had spent more than a generation there, so that their children had no direct memory of Scotland'.[12] In other words there is little allowance here for the very significant fresh Scottish immigration in the mid/late 1690s.

Finally, to return to Northern Ireland and a publication of 2007 by Arthur

Woods entitled *From the Shankill to the Shenandoah: A personal view of the Scotch Irish*, which, like Kennedy's volume, is not academic and thus lacks references. In chapter five, Woods briefly sets out an account of Scottish migration to Ulster and devotes almost all of the text to the reign of James I, suggesting that 'by 1620 at least 50,000 Lowland Scots had crossed the 12 miles of water which divided Scotland from Ulster' and later estimates that 'by 1640 the numbers had reached 100,000'.[13] Somewhat later in the book the author completes his account of the Scots in Ulster with the short statement that 'in the last ten years of the 17th century there was a further 50,000 immigrants from Scotland'.[14] This review of some of the popular literature over the course of the last decade hopefully demonstrates how the dominant popular narrative continues to place significantly less emphasis upon the sizeable majority of Scottish immigrants to Ireland who came during the second half of the seventeenth century.

Moving from a review of the popular literature relating specifically to the Ulster-Scots and Scotch-Irish to that dealing with Ulster history more broadly, we find that the narrative delineated is not greatly different. In 2005, Michael Sheane, as one of a series of recent books on Ulster history, published *Ulster Blood: The Story of the Plantation of Ulster*. In some 130 pages, the author makes virtually no reference to migration into Ulster after the reign of James I. At one point he states that 'immigration from Scotland to Ulster had reached its peak by 1619' and then claims in the book's penultimate sentence that 'it was not until 1633 that the flow of Scots into Ulster became great'.[15] Art Ó Broin, a Munster man who taught history in Derry for two decades, published *Beyond the Black Pig's Dyke: A short history of Ulster* in 1995. Although in the opening of chapter ten, dealing with the establishment of the Protestant Ascendancy, he refers to 'Elizabethan, Stuart, Cromwellian and Williamite planters', the overall tenor of the interpretation is effectively summarised by his earlier claim that 'the troubled nature of modern Ulster was determined by the Jacobean plantation'.[16] The notion, oft repeated since 1969, that the 'troubles' of the past generation owed its origins to the Ulster Plantation inevitably tends to downplay the longer term significance of intervening events. By a distance, the most authoritative and influential modern narrative history of the province is that published in 1992 by Jonathan Bardon. Bardon, in chapter five of this volume, deals with the plantation of Ulster, but attaches the dates 1603–1685, which serves to remind the reader that plantation, in terms of inward migration from Britain, was sustained well beyond 1641.[17] Bardon also crucially acknowledges in a paragraph during the following chapter, the scale of migration from Scotland in the wake of the Williamite war. Nonetheless, it is still worth bearing in mind that Bardon devotes over twenty pages to the phase 1603–41 which saw perhaps 40,000 British settlers migrate to Ireland compared to a mere paragraph dealing with the immigration of roughly the same number of migrants during the period 1690–1715.[18]

An obvious question at this juncture is how did this grand narrative which underplayed the significance of later seventeenth-century British migration take shape? Turning to Lord Macaulay's classic and influential 1849 *History of England*, which also offered regular, if brief, snapshots of the state of Scotland and Ireland, we find a fleeting reference to the scanty harvests which afflicted the former in the later 1690s, but no reference to the sizeable migration to Ireland.[19] The undoubted implication of this trend-setting work is that the colonists of the Williamite era were essentially the descendants of earlier planters rather than recent arrivals. Two highly influential later Victorian histories by Froude and Lecky, though contrasting in interpretation in general terms, did little to challenge the overall impression conveyed by Macaulay.[20] Works relating to the Scot in Ulster and the Scotch-Irish in America in the later nineteenth and early twentieth centuries followed suit in terms of their emphasis on the early origins of the Scottish planter population in Ulster. Harrison, writing on the former migration in Edinburgh in the 1880s and Hanna writing on the latter trans-Atlantic movement at the turn of the century in New York, followed Lecky closely, acknowledging fairly briefly Scottish *migration* in the 1690s but explaining it only in terms of pull factors rather than push, whilst devoting significantly greater emphasis to the migration of the early Stuart period.[21]

An emerging nationalist historiography also paid scant attention to these late arriving immigrants. Neither A.M. Sullivan in his *Story of Ireland* (1867) nor John Mitchell in his *History of Ireland from the treaty of Limerick* (1868) included any direct reference to the Scottish migration of the 1690s.[22] Finally, it is also worth noting the limited attention paid to the 1690s' famine and particularly the associated out-migration, by historians of Scotland from David Hume on.[23] A scan through the 380-odd pages of J.D. Mackie's 1964 Pelican *History of Scotland* reveals no mention whatever of the nation's worst socio-economic crisis and it was only with the emergence of greater interest in economic, social and demographic history in the following decade that the subject began to receive any serious scholarly attention.[24]

Moving to review the academic monographs in this field, we can also see how research and publication has been more focussed on the earlier phase of migration and settlement. In terms of British settlement in Ulster, four volumes have been key to advancing our understanding over the course of the past generation. In 1973, Michael Perceval-Maxwell published *The Scottish Migration to Ulster in the Reign of James I* which makes explicit in its title the terminus date of 1625. A decade later, Philip Robinson published *The Plantation of Ulster: British Settlement in an Irish Landscape 1600–1670*, which sought to extend analysis up to the seventh decade of the seventeenth century. A year later again, Raymond Gillespie authored *Colonial Ulster: The Settlement of East Ulster 1600–1641* and considered British settlement in Antrim and Down up to the 1641 rising. Finally, in 2001, Nicholas Canny produced his long-awaited analysis of British settlement across the island of Ireland entitled *Making Ireland British 1580–1650*, which provided an island-wide perspective, but only up to mid-century. Therefore, none of the major books dealing with British settlement in early-modern Ulster have offered sustained analysis of the significant final phase of migration in the generation after 1670.[25]

In what remain, demographically, distinctly 'muddy waters', let us attempt to map out what we know about the course of British immigration to Ulster during the course of the seventeenth century. The best available estimate suggests that by 1641, Ulster had a British population of something like 40,000.[26] A good deal of the relevant contemporary evidence clearly points to the fact that migration from Britain in the three decades from 1610 fluctuated significantly, but ultimately fell well short of official expectations. At the same time plantation surveys and cartography reinforce the impression that west of the River Bann and beyond the ports of arrival settler population density often remained decidedly low.[27] The compromise with the original plantation stipulations preventing Irish tenants on settler's estates merely confirmed the reality by which suitable British tenants were thin on the ground.[28] Despite the severe disruption caused by war and socio-economic crisis in the decade after 1641, recovery in the two decades following Cromwellian conquest was dynamic and sustained. Fresh immigration from Britain underpinned very significant expansion in British settlement across Ulster. The most detailed research into Ulster's demography in this period remains that undertaken by Bill Macafee for his 1987 University of Ulster Ph.D. Macafee, working from the hearth tax returns, estimates that the total population of the province in 1670 was 350,000, of whom some 120,000 could be identified as British. Thus the British population of Ulster had roughly trebled in the course of a single generation.[29]

Although the expansion of the settler population in the later seventeenth century increasingly reflected impressive levels of fertility within the settled population itself, fresh impetus was regularly added by new migrants continuing to cross the Irish Sea. In the 1670s and 1680s, new migrants from Scotland, England and Wales continued to arrive in significant numbers. The processes of immigration and associated internal migration or colonial spread have been most closely observed in the context of the Lagan valley corridor.[30] A final, very significant and very predominantly Scottish immigration marked the last decade of the seventeenth century, a migration which appears to have gradually, but steadily declined in the opening decade of the eighteenth century.[31]

Contemporary and later estimations of the volume of this *fin de siècle* reinforcement have varied significantly, but it likely that somewhere in the region of 40,000 migrants arrived in Ulster from Scotland between the end of the Williamite war and the opening years of the eighteenth century. Whatever the volume of this final major phase of immigration to Ulster, and we should recognise that we can never establish a precise figure, its importance in consolidating the British, and particularly Scottish and Presbyterian make up of the province's population, is clear. Again, using the hearth tax returns, Macafee offers an estimate for the British population in Ulster for 1712 as being 270,000, just under half of the total population of the province (600,000) and more than double the figure for 1670 (120,000).[32]

Having thus established that, there remains something of a disparity between the chronological scope of the historiography relating to British migration to Ulster and the actual volume of migration, let us consider in a little more detail the relatively ignored, but significant migration of the 1690s. The central reason for such voluminous migration across the North Channel from Scotland in this decade stems from the simultaneous, or at least overlapping, existence of powerful push and pull factors. Ulster exercised a magnetic attraction to prospective Scots tenants in the years after the Williamite settlement. The new security offered by decisive victory in the war was added to by the offer many landlords keen to re-people their estates held out to prospective tenants. In the early 1690s for those seeking to secure a lease it was essentially a buyer's market, a chance to break into the land market cheaply. The falling in of these 21- and 31-year leases and the weaker bargaining position of tenants would later help to fuel trans-Atlantic emigration. Nor curiously does Ulster, a mere thirteen miles away, seem to have suffered the severe famine conditions which afflicted Scotland in the five seasons after 1694. The distress was profound with excess mortality offering a sharp demographic check and stimulating emigration, of which most was directed to nearby Ulster.[33]

Because this migration has yet to be researched in depth by either Irish or Scottish historians, it is difficult to reach firm conclusions about the character of the migrants, but some commentary on this point has been offered by two of Ireland's leading economic historians. As early as 1972, Cullen suggested that the influx of Scottish migrants to Ulster at this time resulted in a significant capital inflow, spurring consumption and assisting rapid post-war recovery in the northern province. However, writing a decade and a half later, Dickson points to something of a transition in the course of the decade when he suggests 'many of the "yeomen" migrants of the early 1690s arrived with some resources, being drawn by the prospect of cheap farms on estates where the former tenantry, Irish, Scottish and English, had disappeared. The later migrants, fleeing from the Scottish famines of 1695–8, were much poorer'.[34]

Some corroborative evidence that these later years witnessed a surge in the numbers of poorer refugees who could be thought of as an external expression of the rise in internal subsistence migrants noted in contemporary Scotland, may be drawn from the evidence relating to poor relief measures in Ulster.[35] In the absence of any compulsory, statutory, national poor law in Ireland, local parish vestries were largely left to deal with the issue in a piecemeal fashion. It is interesting to note something of a rash of activity in this field in the decade after the famine in Scotland. At least six parishes in east Ulster set in motion the operation of a badging scheme to differentiate the worthy from the unworthy poor and allowing them to seek alms within the parish. This, in fact, was a practice common in contemporary Scotland. In 1707, when the County Antrim Grand Jury advocated a similar scheme to be deployed at county level it referred to the 'great increase of vagrant persons and idle beggars'.[36]

To return to thinking more about public history, it is interesting to note how this depiction of the final major wave of Scots migrants to seventeenth century Ulster as famine refugees, so rudely subverts the dominant projection of Scots settlers who are often stereotypically represented as sturdy, hardy, industrious migrants, with means yet seeking opportunities for further prosperity in Ireland.[37] To consider, for example, a classic representation which arguably illustrates a degree of both idealisation and backward projection let us make reference to John Luke's iconic mural in Belfast City Hall. Produced by Luke in 1951, the scene depicts Sir Arthur Chichester reading the 1613 Belfast charter in the heart of the town. The planters surrounding him uniformly speak of prosperity, vigour and godliness as they, somewhat incongruously in 1613, set about the tasks of linen production and shipbuilding. The dominant narrative of proto-industrial and later industrial transformation in Ulster as a direct outcome of Plantation and closely bound up with notions of Protestantism and enterprise, allows little room for poorer migrants who departed Scotland under the threat of starvation and may have been forced to beg alms upon arrival in Ulster.[38]

The shape of Ulster history, long mapped out in the popular grand narrative, also tends to resist revision which points to the late arrival of migrant reinforcements to the Presbyterian church in Ireland. The received version of events portrays Presbyterians who gave their all for a Williamite victory at the siege of Derry and the Battle of the Boyne and were then betrayed by the English interest inflicting the penal laws upon them. Large numbers of Scots Presbyterians arriving on the scene after the war is over and as the legislation is being enacted flows against the tide of written history. Again, reference here to recent popular literature serves to illustrate the point. In 2008, Gary McMurray launched a publication entitled *Journeying Through Irish History* which stemmed from historical awareness

Sir Arthur Chichester reading the town charter in 1613,
mural by John Luke in Belfast City Hall (Belfast City Council)

classes delivered to members of West Tyrone Voice, a group representing the families of security force members killed by terrorists during the course of the troubles. Without any reference to the Scots immigration of the 1690s, McMurray concludes a chapter on the Williamite war and its aftermath with the following passage: 'These Presbyterians, disillusioned that William's crusade for "the liberties of England and the Protestant religion" in which *they* [my emphasis] had fought, had cruelly turned against them, in large numbers fled to America'.[39] Thus the repetition of the long established Ulster-Scots and Scotch-Irish version of this period which stressed the decisive role of the Presbyterian community in securing Williamite victory lead on to betrayal through penal persecution and ultimately disillusioned flight in search of religious liberty in America. Clearly the fresh arrival of some 40,000 Scots immigrants after the siege of Derry, the Boyne and Aughrim, threatened to challenge this account. As Kerby Miller has wryly noted 'it is questionable how many later emigrants were descended from Derry's defenders in 1690, although virtually all claimed to be so'.[40] In this sense it might be seen as particularly ironic that McMurray's book's sub-title was *Exploding Myths*.

One final point worth acknowledging and hopefully thrown into sharper relief by Fitzgerald and Lambkin in their recent survey of Irish migration over the course of the past four centuries, is that migrants from Britain did not abruptly or completely stop coming to Ireland after 1700.[41] Certainly the flow began to decline in scale yet even after the flow into Ulster slowed in the years after 1700 internal migration could continue to push the settlement frontier further south and west. Thus as late as 1714, the Roman

Catholic bishop of Clogher, Hugh McMahon, based at Rockcorry in south Monaghan, could report that Scots Calvinists 'are coming over here daily in large groups of families, occupying the towns and villages, seizing the farms in the richer parts of the country and expelling the natives'.[42] As W.J. Smyth writes, this represented but one of many 'sharp frontiers' being forged along the Ulster borderlands into the eighteenth century.[43] As Fitzgerald and Lambkin seek to highlight, migration across the North Channel, in both directions, had been a feature of Irish and Scottish life for millennia before 1609 and would continue to shape intricate patterns of inter-connection for centuries thereafter.[44]

Notes

1   S. Hanna Bell, *Across the Narrow Sea: A Romance* (Belfast, 1987).

2   Large numbers of US roots tourists wrongly believe that most Ulster Presbyterian emigrants left Ulster for North America in the eighteenth century, whereas significantly greater numbers actually crossed the Atlantic during the Famine and post-Famine decades. A recent and authoritative guide to Scotch-Irish genealogy is William J. Roulston, *Researching Scots-Irish Ancestors: The Essential Genealogical Guide to Early Modern Ulster* (Belfast, 2005). See also Catherine Nash, *Of Irish Descent: Origin Stories, Genealogy and the Politics of Belonging* (Syracuse, 2008), pp 138–81, 244–50.

3   For those interested in pursuing these issues see D. Cannadine, *Making History Now and Then: Discoveries, Controversies and Explorations* (Basingstoke, 2008); in an Irish context see B. Bradshaw, 'Nationalism and Historical Scholarship in Modern Ireland' in C. Brady (ed.), *Interpreting Irish History: The Debate on Historical Revisionism* (Dublin, 1994), pp 191–216. A similar consideration in relation to Unionism awaits exploration.

4   PRONI, D3000/72/1; P.J. McCusker, 'Ballentaken – Beragh in the 17th century' in *Seanchas Ard Mhacha*, vol. 10, no. 2 (1982), pp 487–8; Burke, *Landed gentry of Ireland* (London, 1912), p. 437; M. Rogers, *Prospect of Tyrone* (Enniskillen, 1988), p. 25; www.mcclintockofseskinore.co.uk.

5   M. Rogers, *Prospect of Tyrone* (Enniskillen, 1988), p. 79.

6   See B. Galloway, *The Union of England and Scotland 1603–08* (Edinburgh, 1986); Brian Levack, *The Formation of the British State* (Oxford, 1987); J. Wormald, 'O Brave New World?: The Union of England and Scotland in 1603' in T.C. Smout (ed.), *Anglo-Scottish Relations from 1603 to 1900* (Oxford, 2005), pp 13–35.

7   P. Robinson, *The Plantation of Ulster: British Settlement in an Irish Landscape 1600–1670* (Belfast, 1984), pp 104–08; W. Macafee & V. Morgan, 'Population in Ulster, 1660–1760' in *Plantation to Partition: Essays in Ulster History in honour of J.L. McCracken* (Belfast, 1981), pp 46–64; P. Fitzgerald, 'Black '47': reconsidering Scottish migration to Ireland in the seventeenth century and the Scotch-Irish in America' in W. Kelly & J.R. Young (eds), *Ulster and Scotland: History, Language and Identity* (Dublin, 2004), pp 71–84.

8   For example, on the evolution of the urban network see W.H. Crawford, 'The creation and evolution of small towns in Ulster in the seventeenth and eighteenth centuries' in P. Borsay & L. Proudfoot (eds), *Provincial Towns in Early Modern England and Ireland: Change, Convergence and Divergence* (Oxford, 2002),

pp 97–120; on the migration of Ulster Catholics to more marginal land see M. Elliott, *The Catholics of Ulster: A History* (London, 2000), p. 93.

9   R. Chepesiuk, *The Scotch-Irish: From the North of Ireland to the Making of America* (Jefferson, N. Carolina, 2000), p. 1.

10   Ibid., p. 93.

11   B. Kennedy, *Heroes of the Scots-Irish in America* (Belfast, 2000), pp 153–4.

12   J. Webb, *Born Fighting: How the Scots-Irish Shaped America* (New York, 2004), pp 73, 116.

13   A. Woods, *From the Shankill to the Shenandoah: A personal view of the Scotch Irish* (Glasgow, 2007), pp 37, 89.

14   Ibid., p. 58.

15   M. Sheane, *Ulster Blood: The Story of the Plantation of Ulster* (Ilfracombe, 2005), pp 83, 136.

16   A. Ó Broin, *Beyond the Black Pig's Dyke: A Short History of Ulster* (Cork, 1995), pp 72, 91.

17   J. Bardon, *A History of Ulster* (Belfast, 1992), pp 115, 171.

18   Ibid., pp 115–35, 171.

19   T.B. Macauley, *The History of England From the Accession of James II* (London, 1849), IV, chapter XXII, p. 796. Consulted online at www.gutenberg.org/etext/1468.

20   J.A. Froude, *The English in Ireland in the Eighteenth Century* (London, 1874); W.E.H. Lecky, *A History of Ireland in the Eighteenth Century* (London, 1896).

21   J. Harrison, *The Scot in Ulster: Sketch of the Scottish Population of Ulster* (Edinburgh, 1888), p. 87; C.A. Hanna, *The Scotch-Irish or The Scot in North Britain, North Ireland, and North America* (New York, 1902), I, p. 614.

22   A.M. Sullivan, *The Story of Ireland* (Dublin, 1867); J. Mitchell, *History of Ireland From the Treaty of Limerick* (Dublin, 1868).

23   D. Hume, *The History of Great Britain* (Edinburgh, 1754).

24   J.D. Mackie, *A History of Scotland* (Harmondsworth, 1964); M.W. Flinn (ed.), *Scottish Population History* (Cambridge, 1977) offered the first substantial analysis of the 1690s' famine. In 2005, Karen Cullen completed a University of Dundee Ph.D. on the subject which was published as *Famine in Scotland: The 'Ill Years' of the 1690s* (Edinburgh, 2010).

25   M. Perceval-Maxwell, *The Scottish Migration to Ulster in the Reign of James I* (London, 1973); Robinson, *The Plantation of Ulster*; R. Gillespie, *Colonial Ulster: The settlement of East Ulster, 1600–1641* (Cork, 1985); N. Canny, *Making Ireland British, 1580–1650* (Oxford, 2001).

26   W. Macafee, 'The Population of Ulster, 1630–1841: Evidence from Mid-Ulster' (unpublished Ph.D. thesis, University of Ulster, 1987), II, p. 344.

27   Robinson, *The Plantation of Ulster*, pp 91–108; J.S. Curl, *The Londonderry Plantation 1609–1914* (Southampton, 1986), pp 40–71.

28   T.W. Moody, *The Londonderry Plantation, 1609–41* (Belfast, 1939), pp 185–6, 202–3.

29   Macafee, 'The Population of Ulster, 1630–1841: Evidence from Mid-Ulster', II, p. 344.

30   V. Morgan, 'A Case Study of Population Change over Two Centuries: Blaris, Lisburn 1661–1848' in *Irish Economic and Social History*, III (1976), pp 5–17; R. Gillespie (ed.), *Settlement and Survival on an Ulster Estate: The Brownlow Leasebook 1667–1711* (Belfast, 1988), pp xvii–xviii.

31   S.J. Connolly, *Divided Kingdom: Ireland 1630–1800* (Oxford, 2008), p. 206;
        Fitzgerald, "Black '47": Reconsidering Scottish Migration to Ireland in the
        Seventeenth Century and the Scotch-Irish in America', pp 71–84.

32   Macafee, 'The Population of Ulster, 1630–1841: Evidence from Mid-Ulster',
        II, p. 344.

33   Fitzgerald, "Black '47": Reconsidering Scottish Migration to Ireland in the
        Seventeenth Century and the Scotch-Irish in America', pp 71–84; T.C. Smout,
        N.C. Landsman & T.M. Devine, 'Scottish Emigration in the Seventeenth and
        Eighteenth Centuries' in N. Canny (ed.), *Europeans on the Move: Studies on
        European Migration 1500–1800* (Oxford, 1994), pp 76–112; S. Murdoch & A.
        Grosjean (eds), *Scottish Communities Abroad in the Early Modern Period* (Leiden,
        2005); K. Cullen, C.A. Whately & M. Young, 'King William's Ill Years: new
        evidence on the impact of scarcity and harvest failure during the crisis of the
        1690s on Tayside' in *Scottish Historical Review*, vol. 85, no. 2 (October, 2006),
        pp 250–76.

34   L.M. Cullen, *An Economic History of Ireland since 1660* (London, 1972), p. 29; D.
        Dickson, *New Foundations: Ireland 1660–1800* (Dublin, 1987), p. 45.

35   For subsistence migration in Scotland, see I.D. Whyte, *Scotland Before the
        Industrial Revolution: An Economic & Social History* c. *1050–1750* (London,
        1995), p. 124; R. Mitchison, 'North and South: The Development of the Gulf in
        Poor Law Practice' in R.A. Houston & I.D. Whyte (eds), *Scottish Society
        1500–1800* (Cambridge, 1989), pp 208–14.

36   D. Dickson, 'In Search of the Old Irish Poor Law' in R. Mitchison & P. Roebuck
        (eds), *Economy and Society in Scotland and Ireland, 1500–1939* (Edinburgh,
        1988), p. 151; P. Fitzgerald, 'Poverty and Vagrancy in Early Modern Ireland'
        (unpublished Ph.D. thesis, QUB, 1994), pp 271–80.

37   One should acknowledge that one of the most regularly quoted contemporary
        statements (*c.* 1670) concerning the character of British migrants to Ulster is that
        of Rev. Andrew Stewart, Presbyterian minister at Donaghadee, County Down,
        who described preceding waves of settlers from both Scotland and England as
        'generally the scum of both nations'. However, such assessments represent only
        minor caveats to what A.T.Q. Stewart depicts as an 'Ulster Protestant mystique'
        neatly complemented by the nationalist view, which stressed a belief in racial
        superiority, toughness, loyalty and self-reliance and disassociation from the vices
        deemed to characterise the Catholic Irish: A.T.Q. Stewart, *The Narrow Ground:
        Patterns of Ulster History* (Belfast, 1977), pp 24, 81.

38   The Luke mural can be viewed in the Belfast City Hall. See also Fitzgerald &
        Lambkin, *Migration in Irish History, 1607–2007*, plate 3.

39   G. McMurray, *Journeying Through Irish History: Exploding Myths* (Omagh, 2008),
        p. 56. See also I. McBride, *The Siege of Derry in Ulster Protestant Mythology*
        (Dublin, 1997), pp 23, 57–65 which takes full account of the 1690s' migration
        and serves to chart the later historiographical contestation between Anglicans and
        Presbyterians in both Ireland and America over the siege.

40   K. Miller, 'Ulster Presbyterians and the "Two Traditions" in Ireland and America'
        in J.J. Lee & M.R. Casey (eds), *Making The Irish American: History and Heritage
        of the Irish in the United States* (New York, 2006), p. 269, fn 21.

41   Fitzgerald & Lambkin, *Migration in Irish History, 1607–2007*.

42   Quoted in P. Livingstone, *The Monaghan Story* (Enniskillen, 1980), p. 132.

43   W.J. Smyth, *Map-making, Landscapes and Memory: A Geography of Colonial and
        Early Modern Ireland* c. *1530–1750* (Cork, 2006), p. 463.

44   Fitzgerald & Lambkin, *Migration in Irish History, 1607–2007*.

The Gaelic Irish
and the Ulster Plantation

Raymond Gillespie

The native Irish experience of the Ulster plantation has received little attention from historians. The reason is essentially the difficulty of the evidence. Very few voices from within the native Irish community have been preserved, a result of the essentially oral nature of Irish society. There is certainly a body of poetry in Irish from early seventeenth-century Ulster, but much of this relates to other matters. For example some poetry that has been claimed to shed light on the plantation process such as '*Mochean don loing si tar lear*' was clearly written in the context of the Flight of the Earls in late 1607 and before the plantation was conceived of and hence can shed no light on the experience of plantation itself.[1] Again there is a corpus of poetry in the Irish language that deals with the Ulster Irish in exile after the plantation, of which the best known in Eoghan Ruadh Mac an Bhaird's address to Nuala Ní Dhomhnaill that depicts her weeping at the grave of Aodh Dubh Ó Domhnaill in Rome.[2] While this reveals much about the processes of exile and lament it says nothing about the attitudes of those who remained at home to deal with the realities of plantation and colonisation. Even evidence that appears straightforward needs to be considered carefully and in its context.

The poem '*Beag mhaireas do mhacraidh Ghaoidheal*' by Eochaidh Ó hEodhusa, with its lament for changes in the old order, has some claims to providing an insight into the native Irish experience of plantation, being written in Ulster and *c.* 1613.[3] However, even here caution needs to be exercised. Ó hEodhusa was one of those 'deserving Irish' who received a grant of land in the plantation and in 1603 he had written a poem celebrating the changes that the accession of James I had brought, the brilliant sun of the glory of the king dispersing the mists surrounding the kingdom.[4] Moreover, the patron on this occasion was Brian MacMahon of Monaghan, an area that was not affected by the plantation proper and a landlord who held his own land by royal patent and had been accorded an English knighthood. In this context, Ó hEodhusa's poem can hardly be seen as a reflection of the attitudes of those dealing with the plantation itself. It is better read against another of Ó hEodhusa's poems of 1603, an answer poem in the love poetry tradition that complained of the decline of the bardic order, the decline in literary patronage and the fall in standards in the composition of verse.[5] This motif of 'lapse of Gaelic ways' was common in early seventeenth-century Irish poetry from all over the country, not just in planted or settled areas and a large number of poems reflecting this theme from the late sixteenth and early seventeenth century have survived.[6] The factors behind the decline of the bardic order (and by extension, in the minds of the poets, the decay of Ireland) were much more complex than simple plantation or colonisation and reflect changes in taste and the nature of status consequent on the commercialisation that spread through all of early modern Ireland. Thus '*Beag mhaireas do mhacraidh Ghaoidheal*' is more of a general reflection of the crisis of the bardic order rather than a commentary on the specific workings of the Ulster plantation.

Examining the problems of the evidence and its contexts, only three pieces of evidence in the Irish language can be identified that provide some near contemporary comment on the plantation itself, all of which date form the earliest, most disruptive phase of the scheme. The first is a note scribbled in December 1608 by a scribe working on a copy of Manus O'Donnell's life of St Colum Cille. This copy, he recorded, had been made over the previous year 'in the most troublous year that has come for long in Ireland, especially for us in Ulster and in Tír Chonaill above all'.[7] The second is the entry in the 'Annals of the Four Masters', compiled in the 1630s, under the year 1608. After recording Sir Cahir O'Doherty's revolt at Derry in that year the annalist observed: 'It was indeed from it, and from the departure of the earls we have mentioned, it came to pass their territories, their estates, their lands, their forts, their fortresses, their fruitful harbours, and their fishful bays were taken from the Irish of the province of Ulster and given in their presence to foreign tribes, and they were expelled and banished into other countries, where most of them died'.[8]

As befits a group of scholars led by an exile, Mícheál Ó Cléirigh, the annalists showed little interest in the majority of the Irish who did not travel to Continental Europe but remained behind in Ulster despite the fact that three of the 'Four Masters' belonged to the latter group. The third piece of evidence is provided by a poem of twenty-six quatrains, usually ascribed to one Lochlainn Ó Dálaigh. The poem is undated but its earliest copy appears in the 'Book of the O'Conor Don' compiled in 1631. The poem is built around the rhetorical question 'Where have all the Gaels gone?' and describes the dispersal of the Irish and their replacement with 'an arrogant impure crowd, of foreigners' blood': Saxon and Scots. This appears to refer to the plantation. The poem describes in some detail the religious and landscape changes introduced by the plantation, with enclosures, castles and towns all being mentioned. Poetry and music have vanished and traditional tales are no longer told. At least some of this was traditional imagery associated with the lament for a chief or a past order. For instance, the same motif of hunting woods becoming streets recurs in an elegy for Niall Garbh Ó Domhnaill written in 1626 following Niall Garbh's death in the Tower of London.[9] However, the real reason for these changes, according to Ó Dalaigh, is not the colonisers but rather the judgement of God upon the Irish: it is 'the wrath of God scouring them before all' in the way that the children of Israel had been punished on the Old Testament. The correct response was penance rather than retaliation.[10] This argument was not altogether new. Some years earlier the Antrim poet Fear Flatha Ó Gnímh had written a poem containing almost the same sentiments about the Flight of the Earls. He blamed the flight and its consequences on the pride of the O'Neills and complained that 'No people would have raised themselves above you, O people of the free Niall, if you had been submissive to God who could have overthrown you?'.[11] Thus the correct response to this situation was a return to humility and submission before God.

The problem of lack of evidence is not restricted to texts. The idea of an organised plantation was slow to enter the Irish mentality. Linguistically there was little attempt to incorporate the idea into Irish. The word 'plantation' in its English form appears in a poem usually ascribed to Geoffrey Keating in the 1630s.[12] Only in the early eighteenth century does the form 'plantasion' appear in a history of the O'Rourkes as an attempt to incorporate the idea into Irish. This absence of evidence for the history of the Irish in the plantation means that our understanding of the problem has to be built around records generated outside the Irish-speaking community, both the evidence of government archives and those of the settlers themselves. The picture that can be reconstructed from this evidence works on two levels. From one perspective it is possible to understand something of the ideas about the native Irish that motivated the planners of the plantation scheme and to reveal how those ideas shaped the place of the native Irish in the official plantation scheme.

The Flight of the Earls in 1607 created a power vacuum in Ulster. The restoration of O'Neill and O'Donnell to their lands in 1603 had been intended to create a structure for the government of Ulster, but their surprise departure for Continental Europe in September 1607 left the government bereft of ideas for the management of the province.[13] It did not lack advisers as to what should be done about the newly acquired lands of the Ulster earls. Richard Spert, a veteran of the Munster plantation, urged that a similar course could be followed in Ulster, but said nothing about what this might mean for the native population.[14] Another tract writer grasped the bull firmly by the horns and advocated the wholesale clearance of the Irish and their cattle from Ulster.[15] However, others were forced to face the practical question of the fate of the native Irish in a society with a low population base. For those intending to settle in Ulster there was the immediate law and order problem that the presence of a substantial native Irish population would entail. While the attorney general, Sir John Davies, could play on words comparing the plantation of trees with that of people so that, as with an orchard, the natives and the settlers 'might grow up together in one nation', there was a security problem to be dealt with first.[16] Thomas Blennerhasset, for instance, in his pamphlet of 1610 complained of the problem of woodkerne, or bandits, and even provided a number of clear instances of the problems that they caused but despite this he went on to be a successful Fermanagh settler.[17] The fears created by such publications and oral stories were real and could be played on by both government and other undertakers.[18] However, the paranoia about the law and order problems associated with the plantation needs to be balanced against the widespread assumption that the native Irish would wish to be part of the scheme.

Even the virulently anti-Irish polemicist Barnaby Rich recorded his confidence that a settlement could be created despite all the scare stories he had been told about woodkerne.[19] Perhaps the clearest statements about the expectation that the native Irish and the settlers would reach local accommodations came from the Ironmongers' Company in the Londonderry plantation, who themselves complained about woodkerne activity.[20] Their agent was instructed that he was:

> upon arrival to make publication for all such Irish as will live quietly and manure the ground to entertain, to defend them from the enemy and take no coyne and livery nor cess but what bargain is made to perform the same ... there is no doubt but a great number of husbandmen, which the country calls the churls, will come and offer to live under them [the company] and farm the grounds both such as are of the country birth and others, both of the wild Irish and the English pale.[21]

Certainly by 1616 more than a quarter of the rents of the company were derived from those with Irish names, in flagrant breach of the rules of the plantation.[22] In this case at least, and in many others, there were grounds for settler optimism.

From this welter of advice a scheme for the development of Ulster and the treatment of the native population was shaped. Unfortunately the absence of the privy council registers for much of the first decade of the seventeenth century means that it is impossible to trace how that process

Sir Arthur Chichester, courtesy of the Belfast Harbour Commissioners

evolved. Yet the outline of the government scheme for the plantation and the treatment of the Irish as it emerged is well known. The scheme provided for the allocation of the confiscated Ulster land to undertakers (both Scottish and English), servitors (or government servants, usually former soldiers), 'deserving Irish', and the church and schools. The 'deserving Irish' were allocated some 18% of the escheated lands, more than that assigned to the servitors, but less than given to the undertakers who received 35%, split roughly equally between Scots and English, placing each of these groups on a par with the native Irish in terms of share of plantation lands, although with more estates of smaller size.[23] That the Irish should have received more land than the servitors is a point of some interest given the lobbying by the lord deputy, Sir Arthur Chichester, for the interests of the latter. Servitors, the church and native Irish landholders were free to take Irish tenants on their estates but the undertakers were expected to remove the Irish from their lands, settling them with British tenants. In August 1610, a proclamation was issued requiring the Irish on the undertakers' estates to remove themselves to the lands of servitors, other natives or the church but explaining that they might be permitted to stay, given the low numbers of settlers that had arrived. To ensure the harvest could be saved the older inhabitants were allowed to stay on their lands for a further year.

The following year the removal date was extended yet again until May 1612. By 1618, however, little had been done to remove the, by now, illegal native Irish tenants and the following year an attempt was made to fine those native Irish on undertakers' estates. This still proved ineffectual since undertakers found it more convenient to keep their native tenants and charge higher rents than they might have got from settlers, without the inconvenience and difficulty of finding settler tenants.[24] By the 1620s the Irish were well established on the undertakers' lands and this realisation gave way to a renewed debate as part of the 1622 commission on the state of Ireland as to their place in the plantation scheme and whether they should be allowed to hold leases on undertakers' estates.[25] In reality the prospect of removing them seemed remote. One tract of the 1620s railed against the failure of the settlers to remove the native Irish, claiming that Ulster 'can never be a good plantation' until they did. The Irish, the writer argued were cheaper to find than expensive settler tenants and would pay more rent because they were 'more servile'.[26] As Francis Blundell put it in his discourse on plantations in 1622, the Irish had been left on the Ulster undertakers' lands:

> which being children when they [the undertakers] undertook the
> lands might have been put from them with little or no trouble but
> being now grown men it is worth the consideration of this state
> what course shall be taken with them for I doubt it will be no easy
> work to free those lands of them.[27]

Since the undertakers were technically in breach of the conditions of the plantation, they attempted to regularise their position and an agreement was reached with the government whereby in return for a fine they could retain native Irish on one quarter of their estates, removing the rest by May 1629. However, as with previous schemes, this proved almost impossible to enforce in parts of Ulster and significant numbers of Irish tenants remained on settler estates.

While theoreticians worried about the position of the Irish in the planning of a plantation and how a new social order might be constructed around them, the practicalities of dealing with that emerging social order on the ground had to be addressed in a different way. For those native Irish in Ulster who found themselves caught up in the plantation process at home three main strategies were available. The first was assimilation, that is, the abandonment of any ethnic distinctions and the acceptance of the cultural norms of the settlers by the native Irish. Secondly, there was the possibility of acculturation in which natives and newcomers came together. This meant that there were cultural borrowings between the two groups so that the settlers absorbed some of the cultural markers of the natives, such as language or dress, and natives likewise absorbed ideas and fashions from settlers. The result was something of a cultural melange, with various elements blending together. Finally there was accommodation in which the two groups could exist side by side, tolerating significant cultural diversity with little exchange between the groups. These were not mutually exclusive ways of dealing with the problem of living in a plantation society and all were in play, though perhaps in different mixes over time. Part of the difficulty in understanding how these various approaches were combined over time is the problem in seeing them at work. In some cases, such as assimilation, the success of the process leaves almost no trace in the surviving evidence since successful assimilation, by definition, seeks to eliminate one cultural identity by imposing another, leaving no trace of the older origin of the person. Fully successful assimilation seems not to have been widespread. For instance, there does not appear to have been the large numbers of conversions from Catholicism to the Church of Ireland that one would expect within assimilation. It seems therefore that acculturation and accommodation represent the most common social responses to the plantation process.

In the early stages of the plantation it appears that accommodation or some limited assimilation was a common response to the arrival of settlers. In part this was a response to the fact that in the early stages, the number of settlers was small. The distribution of settler population in 1613, for instance, was concentrated around the main ports of Derry and Coleraine, with little movement into the hinterland, and along the Lagan valley in north Armagh.[28] Large areas of Ulster simply had no settlers with whom the Irish could interact. However, there are signs of the native population becoming involved with the emerging plantation scheme. A case in point is the estate of Sir Claud Hamilton of Shawfield which lay around what is now the County Tyrone village of Gortin. By 1619, there were said to be some fifty British males on the estate, although in 1622, the commissioners surveying the state of Ireland could find no settlers, but 120 Irish were resident there.[29] The latter is a more plausible position.

Before 1613, Hamilton had leased all but five townlands on the estate to a number of native Irish men. Among those the most prominent was one Patrick Groome O'Dufferne (O'Devin). He was one of a number of that surname on the estate and presumably they had been resident there before the plantation. Patrick clearly knew his landlord and was trusted by him and seems to have been forgiven debts in Claud's will. By 1615, Hamilton was dead and his executors appear to have taken the most convenient route for the lands. They leased the entire estate to Patrick Groome O'Dufferne who became responsible for the rent of the lands and presumably collected rents as a middleman from other Irish tenants below him.[30] There are other examples of this sort of activity of using native Irishmen to make settler estates work. The agent for the Ironmongers' estate in County Londonderry, for instance, included payments in his accounts to Daniel O Quig 'for helping to gather the May rent before I came over'. In addition the assistance of the local population was relied on in recovering the names of the townlands and the location of the best building stone.[31] This must have been a widespread process of information gathering which allowed new settlers to understand the geography of their estates and to collect the names of townlands for use in making their leases.

While the rental of the Hamilton estate in Tyrone points to considerable continuities across the plantation, with native Irish being retained on the traditional units of land management – the ballyboe – it also points to significant innovations. The most important of these innovations lay in the legal framework for the habitation of the land. Tenants now held their property by contract rather than by custom. Social relations were now spelt out in writing rather than in terms of mutual rights and obligations within a kinship structure. This drew native Irish into the legal and administrative structures that provided important points of contact between the native Irish and the settlers in the early stages of the plantation, a process that seems to have been widespread in Ireland generally. The Irish language, for instance, contains a significant number of early seventeenth-century borrowings of legal terminology.[32] In the case of the plantation counties it is possible to trace the interaction of native and settler through legal institutions because of the survival, albeit fragmentary, of the records of some courts. Summonister rolls, for instance, record fines levied on large numbers of individuals, both native and settlers, as a result of actions at the quarter sessions. These include fines for non-attendance, for ploughing by tail and whole communities were fined for failing to maintain roads and bridges.[33] Even clearer evidence of the engagement of the Irish with the law is provided by the few surviving gaol delivery rolls of the assizes from the second decade of the seventeenth century.[34] By this date it appears that the Irish were active players in the legal system both as accused and accuser. The rolls reveal the Irish as involved in theft, mainly of livestock, affray and, occasionally, rape and they resolved grievances through the common law process. Perhaps the clearest evidence of the Irish understanding of the working of the law comes with the ability of woodkerne to manipulate the process of obtaining legal pardons for themselves. In some cases they used intermediaries, such as landlords, to obtain pardons for their activities but others managed to acquire multiple pardons for themselves, suggesting that they were at home with the legal system that granted these and were adept at using it for their own ends. In other cases, what appears to have been groups of woodkerne offered to go bail for one another, usually resulting in additional woodkerne activity.[35]

The law was not the only place where natives and newcomers came into contact in the early years of the plantation. While much of the evidence for the workings of local government in the plantation scheme has not survived, a few fragments are suggestive. The proceedings of manorial courts, which enforced the local customary law, for instance, have in the main not survived. However, one set, those for the archbishop of Armagh's lands between 1625 and 1627, are preserved. Admittedly this was an unusual sort of estate and, since it was owned by the church, was allowed to take Irish tenants. The overwhelming majority of the litigants in the archbishop's manorial court had Irish names and among the members of the juries about a third bore Irish names.[36] The sort of cases in which they were involved, mainly assaults and slander, were perhaps typical of local societies grappling with the difficulties of minor rule-breaking and local anti-social behaviour and turning to a local common law framework to resolve these. One particularly important institution in local government was the Church of Ireland parish and here at least some of the native Irish were initially ambivalent rather than outrightly hostile, despite their apparent Catholicism. In the aftermath of an abortive rising in Ulster in 1615, one Cnougher McGilpatrick O'Mullan, a leaseholder from the Haberdashers' Company in County Londonderry, gave a deposition about his very marginal involvement in the conspiracy. In the course of the deposition another episode was recounted which appears to have nothing to do with the plot. A dispute between Art McTomlen O'Mullen and Brian McShane O'Mullen became violent and:

> the said Art uttered these speeches to the said Brian saying, 'Thou art a churchwarden and yet dost not attend thy office according to thy instructions. Thou had sixteen Masses said in thy house by Gillecome McTeige, abbot, to whom thou gavest a white cow for his service and then relievest the said Gillecome and harbourest him in thy house as well as abroad'.[37]

A good deal of the detail here is vague. The identity of Gillecome McTeige is unclear but he may have been the abbot of the Cistercian house at nearby Coleraine, which had recently been dissolved and he may have been living off local charity. The number of Masses suggests that McTeige may have been invited to fulfil some specific task, such as a request in a will for a specific number of post-mortem Masses. Whatever the problems with the details of this evidence, its main thrust is clear: in the very early stages of the plantation process churchwardens of the established church were not necessarily subscribers to the confession of the established church. This may not be as strange as first appears given that before the canons of 1634 there was no requirement for parochial officials to subscribe to any doctrinal statements.

Considering the close linkages between parish and society existing before the plantation it would only be normal that the native population would wish to maintain links with their own parish and to maintain burial and

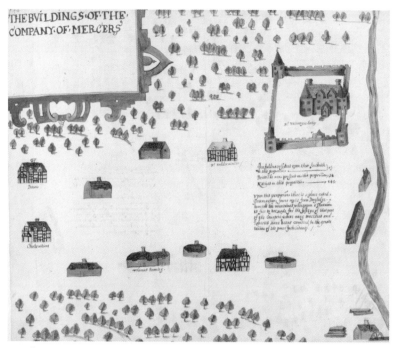

Thomas Raven's map of the settlement at Movanagher, County Londonderry, showing a mixture of housing styles, 1622 (PRONI, T510/1)

other rights in the parish graveyard. This implies an ability among at least some native Irish to differentiate between the idea of the parish as a building block of local society and the parish as a religious community and to participate in one without the other. This has certainly been revealed by studies of parish life in much better documented areas of Ireland. In areas such as Crumlin, on the outskirts of Dublin, for instance, churchwardens continued to be appointed during the seventeenth century in a parish which was largely Catholic and Catholic parochial officials at lesser levels were common in eighteenth-century parishes. Ulster in this respect may not be as aberrant as it is in other areas of social change. In the very early stages of the plantation the idea of the parish may have provided an area of common ground, in which local identities might have been formed.

As the plantation proceeded, the balance between accommodation and assimilation may well have shifted towards the former. There is certainly continued evidence of enduring points of contact between Irish and settlers in the law and other administrative contexts. There appear to have been cultural interchanges at work in the areas of language and dress by the 1640s. As early as 1615, two English servants of Sir Toby Caulfield at Charlemont acted as translators for those interrogated about the plot of 1615 and by the 1640s there were clearly a number of settlers who spoke enough Irish to understand their captors and Irish who had enough English to understand what was occurring around them.[38] Again, in the area of dress there would appear to have been exchanges with an increasing number

Sir Phelim O'Neill

of native Irish men and women adopting English fashions so that when in the late 1640s an image of Sir Phelim O'Neill appeared in an English pamphlet he was shown dressed as an English gentleman.[39] In the area of religion there was also an interchange of ideas so that pockets of native Irish Protestants could be found on some undertakers' estates by 1622.[40] Equally, older cultural traits and agricultural practices survived despite opposition from the Dublin government. Ploughing by tail, for instance, survived and was even adopted by some settlers and the construction of Irish-style houses also persisted, a number being depicted on the maps of the Londonderry settlement drawn by Thomas Raven in the 1620s.[41] The problem with this evidence is that it is impossible to gauge how widespread these processes were. There is one particularly striking piece of evidence that does suggest some measure of assimilation. Some native Irish were sufficiently integrated into settler society by *c.* 1630 to have been mustered as part of the defensive measures of the plantation. Here the evidence is less clear than might be hoped since it rests on the lists of names of those mustered and linking names with ethnicities is an inexact measure. Nevertheless in Tyrone at least six people with apparently Irish names, O'Kelly, McMullan, McGowen, McArt, McGill and McCann, were listed as appearing at the muster, usually with swords or other arms. In Donegal another dozen can be added, including McClearys and McConogheys.[42] Clearly settlers were sufficiently at home with these men to allow them to carry arms, which could be used against the settlers, in a muster. Settlers seem to have been more at ease in other ways too. By the 1630s undertakers were less likely to build the sort of heavily fortified buildings that had characterised the earlier stages of the plantation. Instead they opted for fashion and comfort, putting up structures such as those at Castle Caulfeild or Richhill, with their large windows that were of little defensive use.[43]

Against this evidence for some form of working agreement or assimilation there are indications that in the later stages of the plantation there were at least some Irish who were not as fully integrated into the emerging social order. Such individuals were always there, but are only caught in the sources in generalised ways early in the plantation process as 'woodkerne', living an ambivalent life on the edge of the plantation. By the 1630s, they become more identifiable as figures who were not simply bandits, but were linked to the plantation scheme itself. In Donegal Turlogh Roe O'Boyle, who had received land in the plantation, was said to have been involved with the Spanish in a plot for a rising in the county and again in 1641 he was part of the rising.[44] More shadowy are figures such as Donn Carrough Maguire who was active in Fermanagh in the early stages of the 1641 rising with his brother, Edmund Carrough. Donn Carrough lived on the edge of plantation society. He held land on annual leases rather than for longer periods, that the government wanted people to do to promote stability.[45] In Donegal, for instance, government tried to make landlords responsible for their native Irish tenants, but this proved unworkable since landlords were not prepared to co-operate.[46]

The activities of such fairly well defined marginal figures suggests that there may be a number of forces at work pushing groups apart in the 1630s as well as continuing bonds holding them together. Religion was clearly one factor and the more relaxed attitude to Catholicism in Ulster by the Dublin administration from the 1620s allowed the Catholic Church to rebuild itself in the province and, in doing so, prevent a slide towards the Church of Ireland as a result of inertia among the native Irish.[47] In addition to religion, economic trends served to shape the nature of the native Irish community in Ulster at a number of levels. At least some of those who had been granted land in the plantation scheme as 'deserving Irish' were forced to sell their lands. As the 1622 commissioners observed, one of the defects of the native Irish grantees in the plantation was that 'they do not make certain estates to their tenants but do take Irish exactions as heretofore'.[48] As a result they failed to adapt to the more commercialised world of market rents, fell into debt and were forced to sell their grants. In Armagh, for instance, the percentage of land held by native Irish fell from about 25% at the plantation to about 19% in 1641 and in Cavan the fall was from 20% to 16% over the same period.[49] At a lower social level the dramatic economic growth that characterised Ulster after the plantation meant that the growing number of settlers and the demand for high quality land increased over the first forty years of the seventeenth century and this inevitably reshaped the patterns of settlement on many estates. On the Balfour estate in Fermanagh, for example, distinct patterns of Irish-settled areas can be detected by the 1630s. However, the evidence of the rentals suggests that these were never exclusively Irish and there were always some intermixed settlers.[50] In some places where there had been substantial early settlement this sorting-out process made little difference.[51] In other areas it pushed those Irish who had been left on the estates of settlers in the early years of the century on to more marginal land so that by 1660 some 20% of townlands in the core of Ulster in north Armagh and east Londonderry had no Irish while at the edge of the province only between 5 and 10% can be so described.[52] Some caution needs to be exercised in interpreting such figures since they clearly include the effects of war and dislocation in the 1640s and 1650s but the general patterns appear to be clear. Such patterns of segregation combined with Catholic revitalisation certainly suggest that the levels of assimilation that probably existed in the first two decades of the plantation may have shaded into accommodation in the 1630s.

Despite these changing patterns of response by the native Irish what is most striking about the plantation scheme in Ulster is that it survived for thirty-three years without any significant challenge. At least some contemporaries feared for the fate of plantations. In 1622 Francis Blundell, in the course of a discourse on plantations, observed 'for the Irish being many, strong and malicious and the undertakers so weak, poor and unprovided of houses, arms and means may easily be surprised by them'.[53] Blundell was correct; the native population greatly outnumbered the settlers although there was considerable variation in the distribution of settlers across Ulster. We do not know how many native Irish lived in Ulster in the early seventeenth century. A unique documentary survival for Donegal in the mid-1620s suggest that there the natives outnumbered the settlers by some 3:1.[54] More fragmentary evidence extracted from the undertakers' certificates of the state of their lands furnished to the commissioners in 1622 indicates a varied pattern. In the Londonderry settlement, the balance between native and newcomer was the same as it was in Donegal. In Tyrone things were more closely balanced, with native families outnumbering settlers by only 1.7:1 on undertakers' estates, while in the well-settled baronies of Fews and O'Neilland in Armagh, settler families outnumbered those of the natives by 3:1.[55] The earliest figures that survive on a wider scale are those from a poll money return of 1660.

These suggest that in the escheated counties of Armagh, Donegal, Fermanagh and Londonderry the natives outnumbered the settlers by almost 2:1.[56] No figures have survived from the other escheated counties, but there is no reason to believe that the situation was any different there. However, that population showed little inclination to undermine the plantation scheme. There were certainly rumours of plots, as in 1615 and in the 1620s when English relations with Spain were at their worst, but there seems to have been little substance to these rumblings of discontent.[57] Other evidence of discontent is also hard to find in significant amounts. In both the records of the Ulster assizes and the Dublin court of castle chamber there are few references to sedition or treasonable words being spoken, despite the fact that the Dublin government was alert for such disloyalty. Only a handful of such events, such as the man in Tyrone before the assizes who was alleged to have said 'the king of England was a very poor fellow … and that he did wonder that he should be king of England, for if it should be tried by the histories or chronicles, himself had as much right to be king as he', can be found in the early stages of the plantation.[58]

Equally, in the early stages of the 1641 rising the plantation was rarely mentioned by the insurrectionists as a grievance, according to the evidence of the depositions taken after that rising. While there are relatively few depositions for Ulster in the early 1640s the general pattern of lack of concern for the plantation is borne out by other evidence from the early weeks of the rising. Indeed it was not until February 1642 that the more radical tract, the 'Demands of the Irish', demanded that 'the Scots be removed out of the north of Ireland and the right owners which now beg about Ireland in great want and misery, though of most high blood and birth amongst the nobles of that country' be restored.[59] However, such sentiments were in short supply a few months earlier. When in October 1641, a number of the O'Reillys of Cavan wrote to the government to explain the reasons for the trouble in their region, the plantation did not feature in their analysis.[60] Instead they proclaimed their loyalty to the king, as did most of those Irish involved in the rising of 1641, and placed the difficulties they faced squarely in the 1630s rather than two decades earlier, as well as blaming the 'common sort of people' for the recent violence.

If the rising of 1641 was a conservative affair, seeking not to overturn the plantation process but rather to return Ulster society to the way it had been in the 1630s before the appointment of Thomas Wentworth as lord deputy, it remains to be considered why it was so and why the Ulster Plantation did not provoke a more violent reaction in the province.[61] There are a number of factors that may help to account for this. These might be thought of in two ways: as responses to the potential of violence from above and from below. The most obvious control on the outbreak of violence was provided by the institutions of law and order. Here the provost marshal system that operated in Ulster, and Ireland generally, was the most draconian since it applied martial law even in times of peace. These men were regarded with considerable odium and were regularly complained of for their over-enthusiastic execution of their duty.[62] However, it is important not to exaggerate the effectiveness of the provosts marshal. Like every country in contemporary Europe the ability of a government to coerce its subjects was severely limited by resources. The effectiveness of the provost marshal system depended on the co-operation of local landlords. Such men were often unwilling to assist the provosts marshal against the local population since they had come to rely on the Irish for their supply of tenants. The provost marshal of Donegal in 1626, Robert Cartwright, encountered violent resistance from local landlords when he tried to enforce the laws against wearing Irish dress. Settler landlords threatened him with the law, refused to act against those wearing Irish dress and would not disclose the names of the Irish living on their estates.[63] Clearly more subtle and effective measures would have to be found to maintain social order.

Perhaps more important than these pressures from above in limiting violence were the controls operating from below in checking resistance to the plantation. The first of these were developments in Continental Europe that created a safety valve for discontent. The creation of the Franciscan college of St Anthony in Louvain in 1607 for the training of Catholic clergy provided an outlet for at least some from Ulster who did not want to remain there. Secondly the escalation of military activity in Continental Europe in the years after 1600 meant that the armies were in need of recruits. Thus Chichester proposed to ship Ulster Irish swordsmen, who might disrupt the plantation at home, to Sweden. More important was the army of Spanish Flanders which provided a ready recruiting ground for those in Ulster who felt that they could not tolerate the new order. Thus, for instance, Owen Roe O'Neill, nephew of Hugh O'Neill, earl of Tyrone, left north Armagh as a child and served in the Irish regiment in Spanish Flanders. By 1633, he was commander of his own regiment. A combination of these two element meant that the Irish community in areas around Louvain in the early seventeenth century came to be dominated by Ulster exiles in the army and the church and much of the interest of the Franciscans in Louvain in the history of Ireland and the use of Irish language sources can be attributed to this fact.[64] The escape valve that the Continental armies and the Franciscans provided certainly relieved some of the pressures of discontent in the early stages of the Ulster plantation.

Secondly, and allied with this mechanism for removing potential leaders of insurrection, there emerged, more by accident than by design, a group of native Irish who by virtue of obtaining land in the plantation were given a stake in the existing arrangements. While the Flight of the Earls had removed the most senior members of the great Irish lineages of Ulster, the plantation brought a whole new group of men of the lesser lineages to wealth and prominence by making grants to the 'deserving Irish'. It was some of these same men, including Lord Maguire, Phelim O'Neill and Philip O'Reilly, who were responsible for planning the rising of 1641. They had risen rapidly in the new order, were members of the Dublin parliament, justices of the peace and local gentry, and it was clearly not in their interests to undermine the plantation scheme. Rather their concern was to remove threats to their position that had appeared in the 1630s and to achieve this they appealed to their protector, the king, for support.

At least some of those Irish who became involved in attempted insurrection in the early seventeenth century did so because they felt their newly elevated position in society was not sufficiently recognised. Brian Crossagh O'Neill, who was granted land in the plantation and was involved in the abortive plot of 1615, seems to have become attracted to the conspiracy because he was snubbed at the assizes at Dungannon in 1614 by a Dublin judge who 'was ready to revile me like a churl' rather than the landed gentleman he perceived himself to be.[65] Again Hugh MacMahon, one of the justices of the peace for Monaghan and a substantial landowner, became involved in the 1641 rising because, as he expressed it, one Fermanagh settler 'gave him [MacMahon] not the right hand of friendship at the assize, he being also in the commission of the peace with him' and described the settler as 'proud and haughty'.[66] The plantation created a new gentry group among the native Irish who were jealous of their position in the newly established order and thus wished to protect rather than overthrow the system. Lord Deputy Chichester's argument for giving small portions to many native Irish as part of the plantation scheme so 'that the contentment of the greater number [of Irish would] outweigh the displeasure and dissatisfaction of the smaller number of better blood' would appear to have been correct.[67]

A similar process appears to have been at work, almost as much by accident as design, at a lower social level. On plantation estates there emerged a leasing pattern in which a number of landlords set significant tracts of land to one or more substantial local native Irish persons who then sublet it to others. The case of Patrick Groome O'Dufferne on the Hamilton estate has been discussed above but this practice seems to have been common. On the Balfour estate in Fermanagh, for example, a large tract of land was leased to Irish who sublet it in the 1630s.[68] Again, on the Brownlow estate in north Armagh, a rental of 1635 appears to assign a substantial tract of land around the edge of Lough Neagh, which was later to be the core of Irish settlement of this estate, to John and Garret Barry who would appear to have been Irish.[69] The result was the emergence of a group of substantial Irish tenants on estates across parts of Ulster. These men can be briefly glimpsed in other ways too as local administrative officials. Cormac MacDonnell of Lisnaskea, for instance, was sheriff's bailiff for Fermanagh in 1641 and others fulfilled minor offices such as that of sub-sheriff. Indeed one of the reasons why the local government in Ulster collapsed so quickly in the wake of the rising was the defection of so many minor, yet essential, officials who were native Irish.[70] As with the 'deserving Irish' landowners, such men were given a stake in the new order, with their new found status and prosperity being dependent on its continuance, thus removing the incentive to rebellion.

The treatment of the native Irish in the Ulster plantation was not a simple uncluttered process of government repression nor was the response of those who had to deal with the plantation on a daily basis an uncomplicated one of resistance or acquiescence. There were, on the part of both natives and newcomers, a number of responses that were governed by local and national circumstances and by the balance between aspiration and economic and social realities. There is no doubt that the plantation generated grievances among the native population and that an undercurrent of that can be detected into the 1640s. However, the surviving evidence appears to suggest that it was a minority of those who remained in Ulster, whatever about the views of those who left, who adopted this position. The majority of those who stayed in Ulster appear to have utilised the plantation process for their own ends by assimilating or accommodating themselves to the new order. Indeed, for some of the leaders of that world, the result of their dealings with the new order was such that they felt it worth rising in arms in 1641 to protect their gains, appealing to the king as their protector. Plantations, like many other aspects of life in early modern Ireland, had no simple, pre-ordained outcomes and were capable of generating unexpected and unlooked for surprises for those who were part of them.

Notes

1   Paul Walsh (ed.), *Beatha Aodha Ruaidh Uí Dhomhnaill* (2 vols, London, 1957) II, pp 118–23. For the assumption that this relates to the plantation see Marc Caball, 'Bardic poetry: dispossession and reaction, the reaction of the Gaelic literati and the plantation of Ulster' in *History Ireland*, xvii, no. 6 (Nov–Dec, 2009), pp 243–8.

2   Eleanor Knott, 'Mac an Bhaird's elegy on the Ulster lords' in *Celtica,* v (1960), pp 161–71; Pádraig Ó Macháin, 'The flight of the poets: Eóghan Ruadha and Fearghal Óg Mac an Bhaird in exile' in *Seanchas Ard Mhacha*, xxi–xxiii (2007–08), pp 39–58.

3   Partly edited in Cáit Ní Dhomhnaill, *Duanaireacht* (Dublin, 1975), pp 99–101, 128; on MacMahon, see D.M. Schlegel, 'Sir Brian and Lady Mary MacMahon' in *Clogher Record*, xv, no. 3 (1996), pp 133–43.

4   P.A. Breatnach, 'Metamorphosis 1603: dán le hEochaidh Ó hEodhusa' in *Éigse*, xvii (1977), pp 169–80.

5   Osborn Bergin, *Irish bardic poetry* (Dublin, 1970), no. 30.

6   http://bardic.celt.dias.ie (accessed 25 November 2009).

7   Edited and translated in Paul Walsh, *Irish men of learning* (Dublin, 1947), p. 172.

8   John O'Donovan (ed.), *Annála ríoghachta Éireann: annals of the kingdom of Ireland by the Four Masters* (7 vols, Dublin, 1848–51), *sub anno* 1608.

9   Paul Walsh, *Gleanings from Irish manuscripts* (2nd ed., Dublin, 1933), pp 34, 44.

10   William Gillies, 'A poem on the downfall of the Gaoidhil' in *Éigse*, xiii
      (1969–70), pp 203–09.

11   Brian Ó Cuív (ed.), 'A poem on the Í Neíll' in *Celtica*, ii (1952), pp 245–51.

12   E.C. Mac Giolla Eáin (ed.), *Dánta, amhráin is caointe Sheathrúin Céitinn* (Dublin,
      1900), p. 78.

13   For the context see Raymond Gillespie, *Seventeenth-century Ireland: making
      Ireland modern* (Dublin, 2006), pp 33–44.

14   Raymond Gillespie, 'Plantation and profit: Richard Spert's tract on Ireland, 1608'
      in *Irish Economic and Social History*, xx (1993), pp 62–71.

15   Rolf Loeber (ed.), '"Certyn notes": biblical and foreign signposts to the Ulster
      plantation' in James Lyttleton & Colin Rynne (eds), *Plantation Ireland:
      settlement and material culture, c. 1550–c. 1700* (Dublin, 2009), pp 23–42 at
      pp 40–41.

16   John Davies, *A discovery of the true causes why Ireland was never entirely subdued …*
      (London, 1612), pp 280–82.

17   Thomas Blennerhasset, *A direction for the Plantation of Ulster* (London, 1610);
      John B. Cunningham, 'The Blennerhassets of Kesh' in *Clogher Record*, xvi, no. 3
      (1999), pp 121–6.

18   Raymond Gillespie, *Conspiracy: Ulster plots and plotters in 1615* (Belfast, 1987),
      pp 9–12, 35–7.

19   Barnaby Rich, *A new description of Ireland* (Dublin, 1610), sig B4.

20   P. Robinson, *The Plantation of Ulster: British Settlement in an Irish Landscape,
      1600–1670* (Dublin, 1984), p. 189.

21   BL, Add. MS 4780, ff 69–69v.

22   Ibid., ff 48v–50.

23   Robinson, *Plantation of Ulster*, p. 86.

24   T.W. Moody, 'The treatment of the native population under the scheme for the
      plantation of Ulster' in *Irish Historical Studies*, i (1938–9), pp 59–63.

25   Victor Treadwell (ed.), *The Irish commission of 1622* (Dublin, 2006), pp 157–8,
      162, 179–80, 609.

26   Bod. Lib., Carte MS 30, pp 52–3.

27   BL, Harley MS 3292, f. 41v.

28   Robinson, *Plantation of Ulster*, p. 93.

29   Michael Perceval-Maxwell, *The Scottish migration to Ulster in the reign of James I*
      (London, 1973), pp 344–5.

30   Edinburgh University Library, Laing MS Div II no. 5.

31   BL, Add. MS 4780, ff 32, 38v, 51v.

32   For this wider context of legal borrowings see Liam Mac Mathúna, *Béarla sa
      Ghaeilge* (Dublin, 2007), pp 89–128.

33   PRONI, T/808/15090, 15120, 15126, 15130–5, 15139.

34   J.F. Ferguson (ed.), 'The Ulster roll of gaol delivery' in *Ulster Journal of
      Archaeology*, 1st series, i (1853), pp 260–70, ii (1854), pp 25–9; R.M. Young
      (ed.), *Historical Notices of Old Belfast* (Belfast, 1896), pp 30–39.

35   BL, Add. MS 3827, f. 41; Gillespie, *Conspiracy*, pp 36–7, 41.

36   T.G.F. Paterson, 'The Armagh manor court rolls, 1625–7' in *Seanchas Ard
      Mhacha*, ii (1956–7), pp 301–09.

37   *Cal. S.P. Ire., 1615–25*, pp 54–5.

38   Gillespie, *Conspiracy*, p. 47; Nicholas Canny, *Making Ireland British, 1580–1650*
      (Oxford, 2001), pp 453–4 for Ulster examples.

39   Gillespie, *Conspiracy*, pp 47–8; Canny, *Making Ireland British*, p. 487.

40   Treadwell (ed.), *The Irish commission of 1622*, pp 541, 564, 585.

41   Ibid., pp 512, 514, 519, 520, 523; the Raven maps are reproduced in D.A. Chart (ed.), *Londonderry and the London companies* (Belfast, 1928).

42   BL, Add. MS 4770, ff 77, 85, 90, 92, 94v, 108, 187v, 190v, 200, 203.

43   E.M. Jope, 'Moyry, Charlemont, Castleraw and Richhill: fortification to architecture in the north of Ireland' in *Ulster Journal of Archaeology,* 3rd series, xxiii (1960), pp 97–123.

44   *Cal. S.P. Ire., 1625–32*, pp 382, 383, 393, 396.

45   Raymond Gillespie, 'The murder of Arthur Champion' in *Clogher Record*, xiv (1991–3), pp 52–66 at p. 56.

46   BL, Add MS 3827, f. 62.

47   For this process, see Brian Mac Cuarta, *Catholic revival in the north of Ireland, 1603–41* (Dublin, 2007).

48   Treadwell (ed.), *The Irish commission of 1622*, p. 731.

49   Raymond Gillespie, 'The end of an era' in Ciaran Brady & Raymond Gillespie (eds), *Natives and newcomers: essays on the making of Irish colonial society, 1534–1641* (Dublin, 1986), p. 195; for the case of the O'Hanlons, see Joseph Canning, 'The O'Hanlons of Orier, 1558–1691' in *Seanchas Ard Mhacha*, xviii, no. 2 (2001), pp 74–5.

50   John Johnston, 'Settlement on a plantation estate: the Balfour rentals of 1632 and 1636' in *Clogher Record*, xii (1985–7), pp 98, 99, 102, 105, 109.

51   Robinson, *Plantation of Ulster*, pp 102–03.

52   W.J. Smyth, *Map-making, landscapes and memory: a geography of colonial and early modern Ireland* (Cork, 2006), p. 350.

53   BL, Harley MS 3292, f. 44v.

54   BL, Add. MS 3827, f. 63.

55   Treadwell (ed.), *The Irish commission of 1622*, pp 540–49, 567–87, 624–33.

56   Robinson, *Plantation of Ulster*, p. 105.

57   For the 1615 plot, see Gillespie, *Conspiracy*.

58   Young (ed.), *Historical notices of Old Belfast*, p. 389.

59   J.T. Gilbert (ed.), *A contemporary history of affairs in Ireland from 1641 to 1652* (3 vols, Dublin, 1879), I, pp 382–3.

60   Ibid., I, pp 364–5.

61   For the character of the rising, see Gillespie, 'The end of an era', passim.

62   Gillespie, *Conspiracy*, pp 19–20.

63   BL, Add. MS 3827, ff 62–2v.

64   Raymond Gillespie, 'The Irish Franciscans, 1600–1700' in Edel Bhreathnach *et al* (eds), *The Irish Franciscans, 1534–1990* (Dublin, 2009), pp 48–51.

65   Idem, *Conspiracy*, pp 32–3.

66   Idem, 'The murder of Arthur Champion', pp 58–9.

67   *Cal. S.P. Ire., 1608–10*, p. 358.

68   Johnston, 'Settlement on a plantation estate', pp 97–8.

69   Raymond Gillespie (ed.), *Settlement and survival on an Ulster estate: the Brownlow leasebook 1667–1711* (Belfast, 1988), p. 152.

70   Idem, 'Murder of Arthur Champion', p. 53; idem, 'Destabilising Ulster, 1641–4', in Brian Mac Cuarta (ed.), *Ulster 1641* (Belfast, 1993), pp 107–21 at pp 107–10.

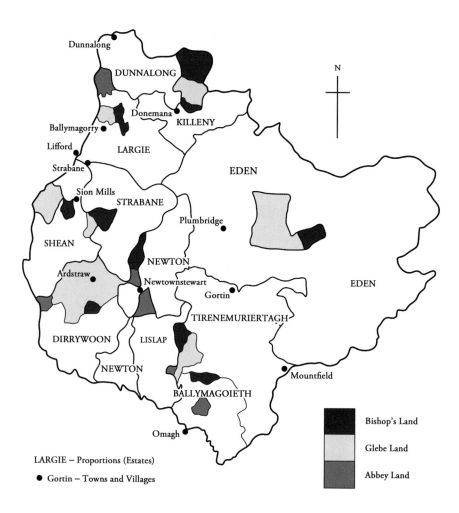

Dunnalong

DUNNALONG

Donemana   KILLENY

Ballymagorry

Lifford   LARGIE

Strabane   EDEN

Sion Mills
              STRABANE

              Plumbridge

SHEAN   NEWTON

Ardstraw   Newtownstewart

              Gortin   EDEN

              TIRENEMURIERTAGH

DIRRYWOON   LISLAP

NEWTON   Mountfield

        BALLYMAGOIETH

Omagh

N

LARGIE – Proportions (Estates)

● Gortin – Towns and Villages

Bishop's Land

Glebe Land

Abbey Land

Map of Strabane barony showing plantation proportions

The archaeological fabric of a manor in the Ulster Plantation: Dunnalong, County Tyrone

William Roulston

In recent years there has been noticeable growth of interest in the archaeology of post-medieval Ireland. This has built on a strong foundation laid by archaeologists such as Oliver Davies, E.M. Jope and Dudley Waterman over the last seventy years. Among the more important recent developments was the founding of the Irish Post-Medieval Archaeology Group in 1999 which since then has organised a series of conferences and published a substantial volume of essays looking at many different aspects of the archaeology of Ireland since 1550.[1] As one would expect, much archaeological attention was, in this volume, as well as in other publications, focused on the official and unofficial plantations of Ulster. It could be argued that of all the academic disciplines, archaeology is the one that has the potential to improve our understanding of this period more than any other. This may seem a grandiose statement to make. However, the surviving documentary record of the plantations is well-worked terrain. The political background to the official plantation scheme has been charted, and the grantees profiled, their land grants identified and their performances assessed. Similarly the processes of colonisation have also been studied and discussed.[2] Where there is still considerable scope for further research is in the social and economic aspects of the early seventeenth century. Raymond Gillespie has considered these in Antrim and Down in his volume *Colonial Ulster*,[3] but there is as yet no equivalent to this study for the six counties that formed part of the official plantation.

While sources such as the muster rolls of *c*. 1630 can provide the names of the settlers, we still know very little of the everyday lives of the British and Irish in the north of Ireland during the early seventeenth century.[4] Here archaeology has its part to play, not simply in the study of buildings and standing remains, but through excavations that can reveal something of the material culture of the period, as well as through explorations of past landscapes.[5] In particular, archaeology has the potential to show something of the revolutionary change that Ireland as a whole was experiencing in the early modern period.[6] This short essay explores the archaeological fabric of one manor in the official plantation and discusses what can be learned about the nature of the settlement created in this locality as a result of this early seventeenth-century scheme of colonisation. The manor in question is Dunnalong. Located in the most northerly corner of County Tyrone, it formed part of the barony of Strabane that was allocated to Scottish grantees, known as undertakers, in 1609–10.

When the settlers began to arrive in the manor of Dunnalong from the summer of 1610 onwards they did not discover virgin territory never before trodden by the foot of man. In fact they arrived in an area where there is evidence of human occupation since Mesolithic times. In general, however, the area encompassed by the manor of Dunnalong is not rich in prehistoric remains, a consequence of the fact that in earlier times it was heavily wooded and in more recent centuries has been intensively farmed. The seat of secular power in period immediately before the plantation was the castle built by Turlough Luineach O'Neill in 1568 on the eastern bank of the River Foyle on a site now within the small townland of Dunnalong. This would probably have been a relatively late example of an Irish tower house. In July 1600, during the Nine Years' War, a star-shaped artillery fort was built around this castle under the direction of Sir Henry Docwra, the commander of the English force sent to the Lough Foyle region some weeks previous to this. At its height the garrison here numbered more than 1,000 men. By the end of the war in March 1603 the garrison was considerably smaller than this.[7]

In 1609 the privy council in London recommended that John Vaughan, a man later to play a prominent role in the development of Derry, should be granted the fort at Dunnalong along with an adjoining portion of land. In the event this was not carried through for in 1610 Dunnalong and its environs was granted to James Hamilton, 1st earl of Abercorn, an important figure at the court of King James VI of Scotland. He was the son of Lord Claud Hamilton of Paisley who had been a leading supporter of Mary, Queen of Scots.[8] In addition to Dunnalong, Abercorn also received lands around Strabane. Two of Abercorn's brothers, Sir George Hamilton of Greenlaw and Sir Claud Hamilton of Shawfield, also received lands in Strabane barony as part of the plantation scheme. The manor of Dunnalong was considered a 'great' proportion, in other words one of 2,000 acres. As such it was reckoned to contain 33 and one third townlands or ballyboes. In reality, Dunnalong extended to more than 10,000 statute acres, all of which lay entirely within the bounds of the parish of Donagheady.[9]

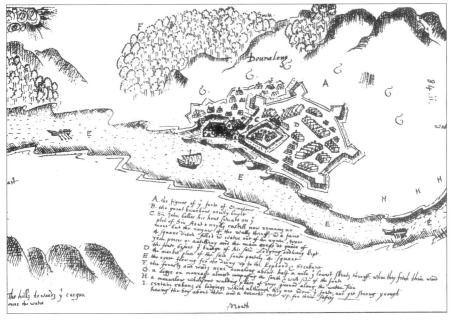

Dunnalong fort *c.* 1601

As a result of the plantation and other settlements, Ulster in the early seventeenth century witnessed considerable activity in the building industry as the settlers constructed a variety of different edifices to meet their needs and, on the part of the undertakers, the requirements of their patents. As a 2,000 acre proportion, the proprietor of Dunnalong was obliged to build 'a stone house with a strong court or bawn about it'.[10] Abercorn was somewhat lax in fulfilling this obligation and there is no evidence that he had made any preparations towards constructing a castle in Dunnalong prior to his death in 1618. Indeed, Captain Nicholas Pynnar noted 'neither Castle nor Bawne' in the manor in a government-commissioned survey of 1618–19.[11] By 1622, however, when another much more detailed survey was undertaken, progress had been made and the official report of the plantation commissioners for Dunnalong noted a 'good Castle of stone & lyme, 3 stories high … and about a Bawne 54 foot long, 42 foot broad and 6 foot high, with two open Flanckers'.[12]

This castle was in the townland that is now called Mountcastle – the name by which the castle is known – but which in the seventeenth century was called Ardugboy (spelled variously). There is no obvious reason why it should have been built here. Though it is now fairly close to the principal road connecting the village of Dunnamanagh with the city of Derry, this does not seem to have been an important route in earlier times. The castle did overlook the large rath at Ballynabwee, and so it might have been an attempt to symbolise the replacement of the old order with the new. However, it is unlikely that the rath would have been occupied in the period immediately before the plantation. A more obvious place to have constructed a castle would have been on the site of the former O'Neill tower house and English artillery fort. Other undertakers at this time were adapting existing fortifications for their own purposes – Brooke at Donegal Castle being a good example – but for whatever reason the pre-plantation seat of power in the area was abandoned.

Mountcastle had been constructed following the death of the 1st earl of Abercorn. Though the report of the 1622 survey attributed ownership of the manor of Dunnalong to the 2nd earl of Abercorn, in actual fact a much more complex arrangement had been worked out. Under a special arrangement of 1620 it was decided that Dunnalong would in time devolve to the 1st earl's fourth son, George, then a minor.[13] In the meantime the countess of Abercorn, the 1st earl's widow, became responsible for Dunnalong, though undoubtedly with some input from her influential brother-in-law, Sir George Hamilton of Greenlaw. According to the certificate drafted by the Abercorns' agent, William Lynne, and presented to the commissioners investigating the plantation in 1622, the man responsible for overseeing the construction of Mountcastle on behalf of the Abercorns was Patrick Hamilton.[14] Among the earliest settlers in the Strabane area, he was a freeholder in the manor of Dunnalong and in

Lynne's certificate and in other documents of the time he is styled 'Reverend'. He is likely to have been the former minister of Paisley, Abercorn's home parish, whose name disappears from Scottish records around 1610.[15] Patrick Hamilton was not the only minister to play an active part in plantation society, but he is the only one known to have been responsible for overseeing the construction of a castle.

The report of the 1622 survey noted that Mountcastle was uninhabited, perhaps because it was not quite finished, but more likely on account of the fact that its owners were living elsewhere. In fact, it is doubtful if was occupied a great deal, if at all, by the Abercorns. The countess lived mainly in Scotland, where she fell foul of the authorities on account of her Catholicism, and spent some

Ruin of Mountcastle, near Dunnamanagh

Old Donagheady church

time under house arrest, while her son, the now *Sir* George, who was granted formal possession of Dunnalong in 1634, resided principally in County Tipperary following his marriage to a sister of the duke of Ormond.[16] The castle was possibly occupied during the 1620s and 1630s in a caretaker capacity by an agent or other leading inhabitant of the manor. Thus Mountcastle was not used for the primary purpose for which it was built.

It has generally been thought that the castle was destroyed as a result of the violence associated with the 1641 rising and its aftermath, and not rebuilt. It seems clear enough that the castle was damaged as a consequence of the rising. The Civil Survey of 1654–6 noted that both Mountcastle and the castle at Dunnamanagh were 'ruinouse'.[17] Whether or not Mountcastle was permanently abandoned after 1641 is not totally clear. In the poll book of Donagheady parish of *c.* 1662, Archibald Galbraith, whose status was denoted as gentleman, appears as a resident in Ardugboy.[18] As noted above, Ardugboy equates with the modern townland of Mountcastle. The fact that he was living here is interesting and may lend support to the idea that the castle there, or part of it at least, was made habitable for a time in the early 1660s. Galbraith may in fact have been an agent for the absentee Sir George Hamilton. Many other plantation castles survived the upheavals of the 1640s and continued in use long after this period. For example, Mongavlin

Castle on edge of the River Foyle in County Donegal was in use as a farmhouse up until the early nineteenth century.[19] Mountcastle certainly did not survive in use that long and was probably abandoned for good before the end of the seventeenth century.

Unlike the impressive ruins that survive of the plantation-period castles at, for example, Monea, Lisnaskea, Tully and Roughan, only a fragment of Mountcastle still stands. Both Oliver Davies and E.M. Jope, writing respectively in 1938 and 1951, mistakenly assumed that the ruins were those of the castle constructed on the Eden-Killeny estate originally granted to Sir Claud Hamilton of Shawfield.[20] This error probably arose from the fact that the report of the 1622 survey was not readily available when they were writing and so the description of the castle at Dunnamanagh on the Eden-Killeny estate found in Pynnar's survey of 1618–19 was incorrectly applied to Mountcastle. Given the proximity of Dunnamanagh to Mountcastle and the fact the no obvious trace of the former castle survives, this was an understandable mistake.

What remains comprises the south-west corner of a building featuring a battlemented bartizan or turret around twelve feet from the ground. Davies and Jope disagreed was on what exactly the ruins represented. As they stand on the brow of a steep slope Davies believed them to be part of the bawn. Jope, on the other hand, argued that the details of the walling from which the turret projected showed that it was part of the castle and not the bawn. The most distinctive feature of the fragment is the moulded corbelling upon which the bartizan rest. Corbelling of this type is a typical Scottish feature and can be found on over a dozen buildings constructed by Scots in early seventeenth-century Ulster. Davies compared the corbelling at Mountcastle to that of the castle at Derrywoon, though he thought it 'less heavy and more pleasing to the eye'. The latter castle, now within the Barons Court demesne, was built by Sir George Hamilton of Greenlaw around the same time that Mountcastle was constructed. As Sir George acted as a guardian for the young sons of the 1st earl of Abercorn and would have had some influence over the management of the manor of Dunnalong, it is possible that the same masons were employed on both castles. The identity of the master mason of Mountcastle is not known, but he might well have been James Miller who was responsible for constructing the castle at Dunnamanagh in 1618.[21]

The bawn around the castle was not large – fifty-four feet by forty-two feet according to the report of the 1622 survey. When one considers the fact that a cricket wicket is sixty-six feet long, it gives an idea of how compact the castle complex must have been. It was certainly not the smallest bawn in plantation Ulster, though many others were of much greater extent. For example, the bawn around Derrywoon measured ninety feet by seventy feet. On the basis of an engraving published in the *Dublin Penny Journal* in

1836 the fragmentary remains have changed little in the last 170 years.[22] Today the ruin stands to the rear of a working farmyard and is visible from the Duncastle Road. That so little survives was probably the result of the castle providing a convenient quarry for building stone for the farmhouses in the area and possibly one or more of the bridges over the nearby Burndennet River.

Further demonstrating their new-found commitment to Dunnalong, a number of other improvements to the infrastructure of the manor had been initiated by the Abercorns by 1622. A stone-built water mill had been constructed. This would have been a corn mill and it was probably located in the townland now known as Milltown. Though, as already noted, no longer the seat of power, the site of the former castle and fort at Dunnalong continued to be important as a ferry crossing over the River Foyle between Donegal and Tyrone. Lynne wrote that a good key had been built there along with a ferry house and 'sufficient boates for men and horse'. Here the annual fair that the Abercorns were permitted to hold took place.

There were no specific rules as to the form of the houses built by the ordinary tenantry though there was an expectation that they would be permanent structures in contrast to the Irish creats which could be easily dismantled and moved to a new location as circumstances dictated. There is evidence that Abercorn attempted to give direction as to the form of the houses his tenants were for build. For example, when William Lynne was granted the townland of Cloghogle in fee farm in 1615 he covenanted to build within four years a 'good and sufficient house of stone and lime or stone and clay with windows and chimneys after the form of Scottish buildings', a unique written example of the desire to transplant Scottish vernacular architecture to west Ulster.[23] Lynne fulfilled this part of his lease for in 1622 it was recorded that he, along with two fellow freeholders, Hugh Hamilton of Lisdivin and James Hamilton of Dullerton, had built 'good stone houses'. A fourth freeholder, Hugh Hamilton of Moyagh, had almost finished building a stone house. As this man had first come into possession of his freehold in 1612, it would suggest that he had been initially living in a timber house.[24] Most of the leaseholders had built houses of stone and the remainder houses of 'cuples', a term implying cruck construction. Patrick Hamilton, the erstwhile clergyman who had overseen the building of Mountcastle, had also been responsible for building 'divers houses of cuples' at the expense of the earl of Abercorn, presumably the late 1st earl.

In direct contravention of the rules of the plantation, which stated that the tenants were to build their houses in close proximity to each other and to their landlord's castle, no nucleated settlement of any consequence developed in the manor of Dunnalong during the early seventeenth century. In fact it was not until the second half of the twentieth century that the village of Magheramason emerged through a post-war housing scheme. In this respect Dunnalong was no different from the majority of early seventeenth-century plantation estates for Philip Robinson has found that on two-thirds of estates there was no nucleated settlement.[25] In the case of Dunnalong the absence of a resident proprietor with his guiding hand would have contributed to the absence of a village. By the time the castle had been constructed in the early 1620s, which might have provided a focus for a village, the settlement pattern had already been established. It must also be acknowledged that the dispersed nature of settlement in Dunnalong and in other districts peopled by Scots was in keeping with the pattern of settlement found across much of lowland Scotland.[26]

While in legal sense the Reformation and plantation did not coincide, in practice the implementation of the scheme of plantation facilitated the extension of Protestantism to west Ulster. The influx of settlers was accompanied by the introduction of a Protestant pastorate and the creation of an infrastructure that would support the reformed church. Although there was a proposal to make each plantation manor equate with a parish, this was not implemented and for the most part the existing network of parishes was continued unaltered. When it came to the provision of venues for public worship, the settlers had a number of choices. One was to repair the existing parish church. This might involve little more than the construction of a new roof or the insertion of new windows. If the building was in too poor a condition to be repaired it might be demolished and a new church built on the same site. There was also the option of building a new church on a fresh site, perhaps in one of the new towns and villages that were in the process of being developed. The decision made in this regard varied from district to district and was determined by a number of factors, including local settlement patterns and the personal preferences of the principal landlord in the area.

In the pre-plantation period there were two centres of religious activity in the parish of Donagheady. One was the parish church itself, while the other was the abbey at Grange. Neither was actually within what became the manor of Dunnalong, but they were both located just outside its bounds. The parish church was situated in the townland of Bunowen. In 1622 it was described as having 'sufficient walls', though lacking a roof.[27] Some time after this the church was either restored or rebuilt and became the focus of reformed worship in the parish. It was almost certainly attacked in 1641, when its minister was killed, but was repaired afterwards and continued in use until 1788 when a new Church of Ireland church was constructed closer to the village of Dunnamanagh.

The ruins that remain today consist chiefly of the west gable to its apex and the lower courses of the east gable with adjoining portions of the north and south walls. With the exception of a small and simply constructed window in the upper part of the west gable, the ruins are utterly featureless.

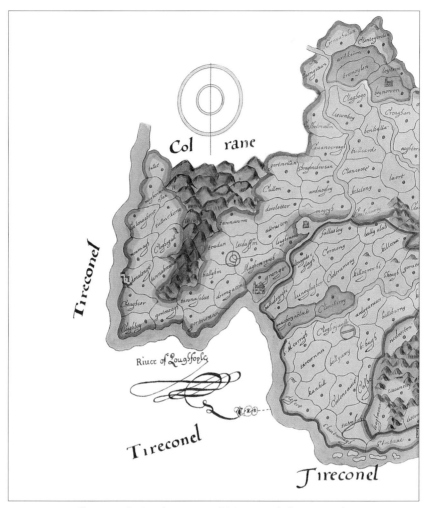

Bodley map of 1609 showing north Tyrone including Dunnalong,
courtesy of the Cardinal Tomás Ó Fiaich Memorial Library and Archive

The door was probably towards the west end of the south wall and it is
known that there was a porch in the eighteenth century.[28] In plan the
church was a simple rectangle with no structural division between nave and
chancel and no tower. In its basic plan and layout the church in the
townland of Bunowen resembled most of the churches used as Protestant
venues for public worship in early seventeenth-century Ulster.

   This reflected a number of issues. The rejection of the need to build a
structural chancel was an indication of the changes in the liturgical
practices of the post-Reformation church. The medieval chancel, separated
from the rest of the church by a large screen, was not conducive to
Protestant worship. Probably of greater significance was the fact that in
Scotland many of the existing country churches were rectangular in plan

and lacked a structural chancel.[29] By building churches on a rectangular plan in the north of Ireland, the Scottish settlers were, by and large, not doing anything different to what they had been accustomed to doing in their homeland. Furthermore, in Ireland as a whole, most pre-Reformation churches were rectangular in plan.[30] When many of these churches were repaired or refurbished by the settlers, no radical alterations were made to their structure. In other instances new churches were built on the foundations of their medieval predecessors. Archaeological investigation has shown that this was the case at Derryloran near Cookstown.[31] The simplicity of the churches was also a reflection of the limited resources available for erecting substantial structures. Church-building was not a high status activity in Ulster in the early 1600s. That is not to say that churches were not patronised by the elite. Certainly they were and were it not for the contribution of the landowning classes, many parishes would be without any church. However, for the most part the new landlords did not lavish money on building architecturally distinguished churches.

Though its origins are not known for certain – and there is a marked lack of local tradition associated with it – the abbey at Grange possibly originated as a Patrician foundation. It was certainly in existence by the late medieval period when it was associated with the Augustinian order and attached to the Black Abbey, or Dub Regles, in Derry. The abbey is pictorially represented on Bodley's map of 1609 though this cannot be taken as accurately representing its appearance. How substantial the monastic buildings were is not clear and one must have grave reservations about the accuracy of the statement in Lewis' *Topographical Dictionary* (1837) that the ruins were 'extensive', especially as they are not marked on the contemporary first edition Ordnance Survey map of the area. A significant proportion of the former abbeylands were reclaimed in the course of the nineteenth century in the pursuit of agricultural improvement, but even at the beginning of the seventeenth century there would have been a sizeable acreage of good quality arable land associated with the abbey. Having been confiscated at the time of the plantation at the beginning of the seventeenth century, the abbeylands passed through a series of owners before coming into the possession of Hugh Hamilton of Lisdivin. In 1638, these lands were divided with the portion known as Drummeny going to Hugh Hamilton's cousin, confusingly another Hugh Hamilton.[32]

Though Grange was no longer used as a religious house, the burial ground adjoining the abbey was appropriated by the local settler community and used as their place of interment. As such it continued to be the chief place of burial for the local population until the 1930s when it was closed because of overcrowding. One gravestone, however, managed to survive from the early seventeenth century. This commemorates Robert

Tombstone to Robert Granger (d. 1630), Grange graveyard

Granger, a Scottish planter, who died in 1630. In the certificate presented
to the commissioners in 1622 Granger is listed among the leaseholders in
the manor of Dunnalong. From another source we know that he lived in
the townland of Cloghboy.[33] As was the general practice at the time, the
inscription on this gravestone runs around the margins of the ledger.
Though damaged, Granger's name and the date are clearly legible as is the
name of the deceased's wife, Kathren Hill. R.J. Hunter has explored the
significance of this memorial in his very fine chapter in *Tyrone: History and
Society* and makes the point that it represents an 'essentially familial
conception of a memorial' in that its primary purpose was to commemorate
the deceased and his family.[34] The stone's only decoration is a heraldic
shield featuring three stags' heads. Here we see an attempt to signify the
family's status and place in society. This was particularly important in early
seventeenth-century settler society in Ulster where the newcomers had no
roots and where the traditional networks and bonds that defined one's
position in England and Scotland were absent. In these circumstances the
identification of a place of burial became all the more important. Such

concerns can also be seen on the roughly contemporaneous memorial in nearby Old Leckpatrick graveyard which reads, 'Here is the burial place of John Maghee who deseased 26 February 1617 and his family'.

The foregoing study has shown that Dunnalong is not a plantation manor rich in archaeological remains, a fact which presents challenges for studying the process of societal change in this locality during this formative period. It does not boast a castle of the magnitude of Monea or a place of worship comparable to the fine early seventeenth-century church still in use in Benburb. Neither is there a field in which the grass-grown contours of a lost plantation village can be discerned. Nonetheless, it is possible to glimpse into the worlds of those who attempted to shape this district in the early seventeenth century even if the view is much obscured. In many ways Dunnalong fell far short of the ideal that the promoters and devisers of the official plantation scheme had in mind in the years leading up to 1610. The model of ordered settlement focused on a lordly residence with adjoining village did not operate in Dunnalong. But then neither did it in most plantation manors, a reality that highlights quite clearly the contrast between, on the one hand, the theory of plantation, and, on the other, what actually happened on the ground. That the early modern period was a time of immense change in Ireland is incontrovertible. By fully integrating archaeology to the interdisciplinary study of this period, we will have a much fuller picture of the processes and implications of that change.

Notes

1   Audrey Horning, Ruairí Ó Baoill, Colm Donnelly & Paul Logue (eds), *The Post-Medieval Archaeology of Ireland, 1550–1850* (Dublin, 2007).

2   G. Hill, *An historical account of the plantation in Ulster at the commencement of the seventeenth century* (Belfast, 1877); M. Perceval-Maxwell, *The Scottish migration to Ulster in the reign of James I* (London, 1973); Philip Robinson, *The Plantation of Ulster* (Dublin, 1984); N. Canny, *Making Ireland British, 1580–1650* (Oxford, 2001).

3   Raymond Gillespie, *Colonial Ulster: the settlement of east Ulster, 1600–1641* (Cork, 1985).

4   Recently published as R.J. Hunter (ed.), *'Men and arms': the Ulster settlers, c. 1630*, prepared for publication by John Johnston (Belfast, 2012).

5   Nick Brannon, 'Archives and archaeology: the Ulster plantations in the landscape' in G. Egan & R.L. Michael (eds), *Old and New Worlds* (Oxford, 1999), pp 97–105.

6   Raymond Gillespie, 'Material culture and social change in early modern Ireland' in James Lyttleton & Colin Rynne (eds), *Plantation Ireland: settlement and material culture, c. 1550–c. 1700* (Dublin, 2009), pp 53–60.

7   W.J. Roulston, *The parishes of Leckpatrick and Dunnalong: their place in history* (Letterkenny, 2000), pp 15–29.

8   Perceval-Maxwell, *Scottish migration*, pp 325–7.
9   W.J. Roulston, 'The Ulster Plantation in the manor of Dunnalong, 1610–70' in
     H.A. Jefferies & C. Dillon (eds), *Tyrone: History and Society* (Dublin, 2000),
     pp 267–90 at p. 268.
10   T.W. Moody, 'The revised articles of the Ulster plantation' in *Bulletin of the
     Institute of Historical Research*, xii (1934–5), pp 178–83.
11   Hill, *Plantation in Ulster*, p. 529.
12   Victor Treadwell (ed.), *The Irish commission of 1622* (Dublin, 2006), p. 568.
13   *Calendar of the patent rolls of the reign of James I* (rpr. Dublin, 1966), p. 471.
14   Huntingdon Library and Archives, Kimbolton MS DDM 70/35.
15   W.M. Metcalfe, *A history of Paisley, 600–1908* (Paisley, 1909), p. 213.
16   Conleth Manning, 'The two Sir George Hamiltons and their connections with
     the castles of Roscrea and Nenagh' in *Tipperary Historical Journal* (2000),
     pp 149–54.
17   R.C. Simington (ed.), *The Civil Survey III* (Dublin, 1937), p. 395.
18   PRONI, T/1365/1.
19   *Dublin Penny Journal*, vol. 4, no. 186 (23 Jan. 1836), p. 240.
20   Oliver Davies, 'Mountcastle' in *Ulster Journal of Archaeology*, 3rd series, 1 (1938),
     pp 215–16 at p. 215; E.M. Jope, 'Scottish influences in the north of Ireland:
     castles with Scottish features, 1580–1640' in *Ulster Journal of Archaeology*, 3rd
     series, 14 (1951), pp 31–47 at p. 43.
21   PRONI, T/544.
22   *Dublin Penny Journal*, vol. 4, no. 186 (23 Jan. 1836), p. 240.
23   PRONI D/623/B/13/1.
24   PRONI, LPC/1367.
25   Robinson, *Plantation of Ulster*, p. 158.
26   I. Whyte, *Agriculture and society in seventeenth-century Scotland* (Edinburgh, 1979),
     pp 21–4.
27   PRONI, DIO/4/23/1/1.
28   PRONI, MIC/1/35.
29   Deborah Howard, *Scottish architecture from the Reformation to the Restoration,
     1560–1660* (Edinburgh 1995), pp 175–7.
30   R. Stalley, 'Irish Gothic and English fashion' in J. Lydon (ed.), *The English in
     Medieval Ireland* (Dublin, 1984), pp 65–86 at pp 67–8.
31   Colm Donnelly, *Living Places* (Belfast, 1997), p. 110.
32   Roulston, *Parishes of Leckpatrick and Dunnalong*, p. 43.
33   PRONI, T/808/15090.
34   R.J. Hunter, 'Style and form in gravestone and monumental sculpture in County
     Tyrone in the seventeenth and eighteenth centuries' in Jefferies & Dillon (eds),
     Tyrone: History and Society, pp 291–326 at pp 291–4.

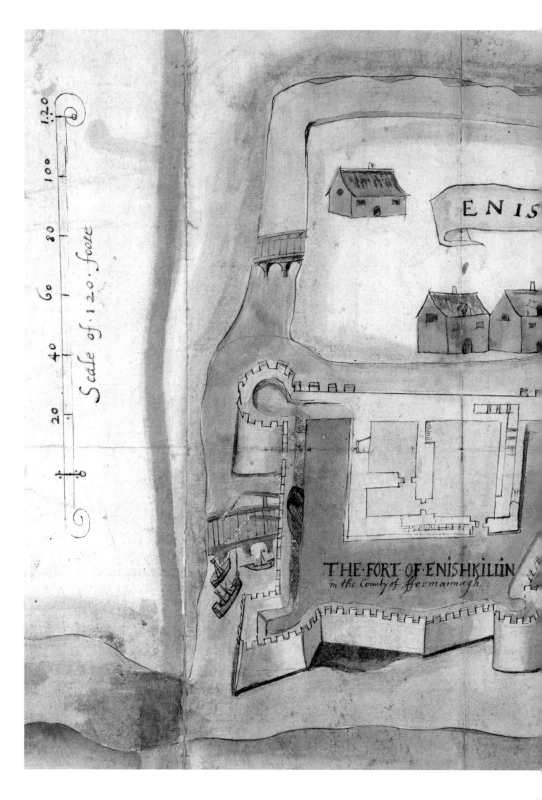

Scale of 120 foote

120
100
80
60
40
20

ENIS

THE·FORT·OF·ENISHKILLIN
in the County of ffermannagh

Plan of Enniskillen
c. 1611, courtesy of
the Board of Trinity
College Dublin

Enis Kelling Fort

Lough Earne

Detail of Enniskillen fort in John Speed's map of Ulster published in
The Theatre of the Empire of Great Britaine, 1612, courtesy of the
Cardinal Tomás Ó Fiaich Memorial Library and Archive

From the Broads to the Lakelands – English plantation in Fermanagh

John Cunningham

To give a very simplified mental picture of the plantation of Fermanagh one must visualise the county as a rectangle, with Lough Erne running from east to west through the centre of the county. South of this east-west line are three of the seven baronies of Fermanagh, with the most easterly and the most westerly, namely Knockninny and Magheraboy, granted to Scottish settlers and the central one partly to native Irish and partly to English. On the northern side of the Erne, the two baronies, at either end of Fermanagh, were granted to English settlers and the two central baronies largely to Irish natives other than around Enniskillen which was to be the new centre of the county of Fermanagh.

The south-eastern barony originally granted to Scots from around the Edinburgh area collapsed within the first ten years of the plantation. By 1619, Sir Stephen Butler, an Englishman from Bedfordshire, had purchased 8,000 of the 9,000 acres granted initially to the Scots, rendering this barony rather more English than Scottish almost straightaway. So now the English held almost four of the seven baronies of Fermanagh, the most strategic places in the county: in the west next to the sea at Ballyshannon; in the centre about Enniskillen; and in the east close to the entrance to the Upper Erne with its overland links to Dublin.

Most of the English who arrived in Fermanagh came from the area of East Anglia, generally as undertakers – those who undertook to carry out various conditions in the areas which they planted, such as the building of a castle and bawn enclosure and the building of a church. To do this they had to have a certain high level of income (self-assessed) to build and to attract from England sufficient quality settlers to labour and farm and occupy the territory granted. The majority of the servitors who received land in Fermanagh were also English. In the barony of Clinawley, Sir John Davies, attorney general, received 1,500 acres in the rich wheat-bearing district around Lisgoole Abbey and reaching towards Enniskillen. Samuel Harrison received 500 acres and Peter Mostyn from Flintshire was granted 246 acres.

The baronies of Coole and Tirkeneda contained 116,006 acres almost entirely occupied by nine undertakers, four of whom were servitors. These were Sir Henry Ffolliott, Baron Folliott of Ballyshannon, (1,500 acres), Roger Atkinson, (1,000 acres), William Cole, reputedly from Devon, (1,000 acres), and Paul Gore, son of a merchant-tailor of London, who had 1,348 acres, called the manor of Inishmore.

In this short essay, I am trying to explore why these English people were coming to Ireland when at the same time their neighbours, particularly in East Anglia, were making America their plantation destination choice. Why Fermanagh rather than Jamestown in America, named after King James I? After all, most of the inhabitants of America's first permanent English settlement came from Norfolk, England, including Samuel Lincoln, a forefather of President Abraham Lincoln.

Firstly, by the early seventeenth century, the English had gained considerable knowledge about this part of Ireland while relatively little was known of the Americas. Quite a few events of the Nine Years' War had taken place in and around the Erne. In 1597, the English were defeated at Ballyshannon and then there had been a major siege of Enniskillen Castle in 1594. The island on which Enniskillen is built was captured by the English in 1607 and Ballyshannon had received a Royal Charter in 1613. So those who had served in the English army in Ireland and who as English servitors were to be rewarded with Irish lands knew Fermanagh well and probably liked the economic potential of its dense forests to produce charcoal to smelt the local low grade iron, its fertile soil and its teeming fisheries.

Sir John Davies, a chief architect of the plantation, wrote after visiting Fermanagh:

> Have now finished in Fermanagh, which is so pleasant and fruitful a country that if he should make a full description thereof it would rather be taken for a poetical fiction, than for a true and serious narration. The fresh lake called Lough Erne being more than 40 miles in length, and abounding in fresh water fish of all kinds, and containing 100 dispersed islands, divides that county into two parts; the land on either side of the lough rising in little hills of 80 or 100 acres apiece, is the fattest and richest soil in all Ulster.

He went on to suggest planting Dutch people in Fermanagh, also led by a Dutch merchant called Maximilian van der Lever, who, 'by their industry the lake will be so full of boats and barks, that they will be a great strength to all the civil inhabitants round about'.

The Dutch interest in Fermanagh came to naught, but it too had an origin in East Anglia. For centuries there had been huge commercial links between the Low Countries and this part of England. Dutch Protestant refugees fleeing Spanish Catholic persecution in their own country were gaining refuge in East Anglia much to the annoyance of the Spanish. When the English upbraided the Spanish for giving refuge to the Irish earls who fled there they responded in turn by pointing out England's acceptance of Dutch refugees.

Such was the English interest in Fermanagh that they actually petitioned to plant the entire county themselves. The names of forty gentlemen are recorded who offered to bestow £40,000 on the plantation of Fermanagh as they 'intend to have a market town on the south side thereof at Bellike, and from thence, three miles nearer the sea, to erect a strong corporation at Ballyshannon'. They intended to erect forty manors, if they were granted 60,000 acres, 'the Loughe, Islands therein, Fishings, and the sole command thereof and they with followers, not less than 1000 men well furnished for all kind of handiwork'. Of those forty listed, twenty-two came from Norfolk and Suffolk and the rest from adjoining counties, from London or were already in Ireland, possibly with contacts to the same area.

In the precinct of Lurg and Coolemakarnan in north-west Fermanagh, 9,000 acres were allocated mainly to men of Norfolk and Suffolk. 1,000 acres were granted to Thomas Flowerdewe, John Archdale, (Suffolk), Edward Warde, Thomas Barton, (Norfolk) and Henry Honynge, (Suffolk). John Archdale was related through marriage to the Honynge family having married Francis Hoynynge. The last two were portions of 2,000 acres each to Thomas Blennerhassett, Esq., Norfolk, and Sir Edward Blennerhassett of the same place. The Blennerhassetts built what is now known as Crevenish Castle, near Kesh, which they called Castlehasset and established English workmen and tenants about them whom they brought from their home near Norwich.

Before becoming established in East Anglia, the Blennerhassetts had lived in a village of the same name in Cumberland, about twenty miles to the southwest of the city of Carlisle. The village of Blennerhassett today consists of a pub, post office and a village school with a small scattering of houses and their toponomic derives from this location. Previous generations of the family who had lived on the Cumbrian coast just a short distance from Ulster also had a familiarity with Ireland; these included the related Blennerhassetts who had set themselves up in County Kerry area shortly before, around Blennerville, where they are still to be found today. These large grants of land had come from Queen Elizabeth I when the earl of Desmond's estates were forfeited and so the family had a familiarity with the idea of plantations before they ever came to Fermanagh.

Thomas Blennerhassett's career before coming to Ireland included being captain of Guernsey Castle. He was a literary man and wrote several books including a volume entitled *Directions for the Plantation of Ulster*. He also issued a proclamation as a form of advertising to encourage others in the task of bringing 'civilization' to Ireland. In part it reads:

> The County of Fermanagh, sometimes Maguire's County rejoice. Many undertakers, all incorporated in mind as one, they, there with their followers, seek and are desirous to settle themselves. The islands of Lough Erne shall have habitations, a fortified corporation, market towns and many new erected manors, shall now so beautify her desolation that her inaccessible woods, with spaces made tractable, shall no longer nourish devourers, but by the sweet society of a loving neighbourhood, shall entertain humanity even in the best fashion. Go on worthy Gentlemen, fear not, the God of Heaven will assist and protect you.

Thomas Blennerhassett in 1611 was reported by Gatisfeth, one of the inspectors of the progress of the plantation, to have with him six persons, one a joiner, another a carpenter, and three other workmen, with one tenant.

> He has built a boat, and has broken stones for lime and some burnt; and thirty trees felled; some squared and sawed; a fair large Irish house, with windows and rooms after the English manner, wherein is a new kitchen with a stone chimney and an oven. For cattle three horses, a mare and some thirteen head of other cattle.

There were two principal ways of generating wealth in Fermanagh in this early period of the plantation; smelting low grade iron ore and the making of barrel staves. Both Blennerhassetts built iron works at Clonelly and Hassetts Fort which is now Castle Caldwell near Belleek, while there was another nearby at Garrison. Gerard Boate's *Natural History of Ireland*, written 'for the benefit of adventurers and planters', indicates that woodcutters were needed, sawyers to saw, carpenters, masons, smiths, bellow makers, water leaders or water-course keepers to steer the water course, bucket makers to make containers for carrying ore and other materials, diggers of ore, carriers of ore, colliers to make charcoal, fillers to put ore and charcoal into the furnace, furnace keepers, firers and hammerers to look after the smelted iron and labourers to look after anything else: 'and for all this, the owners thereof did greatly gain thereby, ordinarily not less than forty in the hundred per annum'. According to Boate, 'Iron works were a very profitable if highly destructive industry. Most of the Fermanagh produced iron being exported via Ballyshannon at

£11 per ton and fetching £17 per ton in London'. In those days the favourite objects of solicitude were the manufacture of pipe-staves, and the development of the iron-works which were then supposed to be the true El Dorado of Irish enterprise – most people holding with Francis Bacon, 1st Viscount Saint Albans (1561–1626) that 'Iron is a brave commodity where wood aboundeth'. Both industries depended for their success upon the woods, which were accordingly drawn upon regardless of the consequences. From Munster, whole shiploads of pipe-staves were exported, to the great profit of the proprietors and the great destruction of the woods; and Boate says, in his *Ireland's Naturall History*, 'it is incredible what quantity of charcoal is consumed by one iron-work in a year'. These enterprises were carried on at a terrible price to the Irish landscape. This wholesale deforestation began the process which has resulted in Ireland being one of the least forested countries of Europe, with only about 9% of the country covered in trees, while France, for example, has about 40% forest cover.

In summary, the vast majority of Fermanagh was planted by either English undertakers or servitors, many of whom had an intimate knowledge of the area from their military experience or previous contact as planters in Ireland. They knew that with plentiful forests they could make money from smelting iron or converting the forests into usable timber, particularly barrel staves. They brought in numerous English settlers, whose names are still found in the county – Barton, Archdale, Allingham, Cole, Chittick, Eves and even a solitary Blennerhassett. Fermanagh history needs to be rewritten to take account of this English aspect of its heritage.

I have been in East Anglia numerous times to visit its libraries and public record offices and have been struck by the lack of records dealing with the movement of people from East Anglia to Fermanagh. There are shipping lists of those going to Jamestown, down to the last commoner, but nothing about plantation families going to Ireland. Perhaps the overwhelming fame of America has totally eclipsed the memory of those who went to Ireland.

My particular interest in the plantation period concerns the name of Eves, an East Anglian name from Old English, meaning a dweller beside a forest. Three of that name came to Fermanagh with the Archdales, as ploughmen. An Eleanor Eves is noted in the 1821 census fragment for County Fermanagh as a lady's maid to the wife of General Archdale. Unusually, perhaps the Eves family remained Roman Catholic, despite being closely allied with, and working for, the landed Archdales who were Church of Ireland. It has been noted in the predominantly Protestant Kesh area that through the centuries the Eves could purchase any property in the locality, despite their religion in a largely Protestant neighbourhood – presumably under the benevolent wing of the Archdales – and they also were the operators of one of the first post offices in the village of Kesh. As one might say, old family links from the Broads of East Anglia were maintained in the lakelands of County Fermanagh.

The 1622 royal visitation of the Church of Ireland in Ulster

Brendan Scott

In 1622, a report from the Irish Commission of that year, entitled 'Certificate concerning the church government in Ireland', was compiled.[1] As can be discerned from the document's title, it dealt with the state of the Church of Ireland and much of it made depressing reading for King James I and his council, who were hoping to reform the religious views of the Catholic Gaelic Irish and Old English communities throughout Ireland. The conclusions made by the commissioners in their report come from the regal visitation of the Church of Ireland held throughout Ireland that year. According to the commissioners, the appropriation of church property by the lay community was carried out on a grand scale, Church of Ireland curates' fees were often at the discretion of Catholic laymen, Catholic chantries[2] were still open, members of the Catholic lay community dodged the payment of tithes, and many of the clergy were neither capable nor inclined to carry out the reforms required by the Church of Ireland. This report, somewhat ignored at the time, lay fallow until the 1630s when it prepared the groundwork for much of the religious policies undertaken by Lord Deputy Wentworth and Bishop John Bramhall of Derry.[3]

The returns from the 1622 regal visitation of the Church of Ireland are an extremely important, yet somewhat neglected, source for those interested in ecclesiastical and social history in early seventeenth-century Ireland. This paper will discuss how the results of this visitation highlight the problems and abuses prevalent in the Church of Ireland in Ulster in the early seventeenth century and how these contributed to its failure to win over the Gaelic Irish and Old English to the reformed faith.

A commission was appointed in 1622 'to enquire into the state ecclesiastical and temporal of Ireland'. This resulted in what has been described as a 'wealth of certificates, notes on various subjects and the commissioners' recommendations thereon'.[4] The commission itself had been established as a result of fears dating from mid 1621 and shared by the English parliament and monarchy that a vulnerable Ireland could be exploited, either by foreign powers and/or a discontented nobility and gentry in Ireland, wishing to destabilise British power there. It was also felt by the earl of Middlesex, the lord treasurer, among others, that a weakly governed or discontented Ireland was a burden too many on the Stuart crown finances, as had also been the case during the Tudor period. It has recently been estimated that Ireland was costing the crown about £47,170 per annum, money which the state felt could be put to better use elsewhere.[5] Therefore, the decision was made to make a far-reaching enquiry into the state of Ireland, both civil and ecclesiastical.

The commissioners began their work in April 1622, when they requested of the bishops of the Church of Ireland a complete and thorough account of their clergy and livings.[6] Once completed, the bishop's findings were sent to the commissioners, who studied them and cited them in their general report of the church mentioned above.[7] Although the bishops complied, what they submitted varied greatly, both in quantity and quality. James Ussher, for example, then bishop of Meath and Clonmacnoise, which is part of the archbishopric of Armagh, submitted a massive report on his united dioceses. The surviving report submitted by Bishop Edward King for the diocese of Elphin, however, runs to a paltry four folios.

All of the Ulster returns, bar Dromore, survive in their earliest extant form in Manuscript 550 now in the care of Trinity College Dublin. Ossory is the only original certificate which survives – those in Trinity College are close contemporaries, but not originals. The eventual fate of the rest of the originals is not known – they seem to have been delivered to Lambeth Palace Library and later passed into the hands of John Selden, the seventeenth-century antiquarian. Following Selden's death, it is likely that his executor, Matthew Hall, took possession of them. Another seventeenth-century antiquarian, James Ware, also held them for a time but their fate after this is unknown.[8]

One important power which the commission possessed was the right to negotiate with impropriators of church livings for larger stipends to ministers of livings in their care.[9] This demonstrates the awareness on the part of the commissioners of a major stumbling block in the introduction of the reformed religion into Ireland – so long as lay people, especially conservatives, held church advowsons,[10] no real move could be made to introduce reform-minded, educated ministers into what were relatively poor livings.[11] Furthermore, as they negotiated this clause themselves, it demonstrated the will on the commissioners' part to attempt a root and branch reform of the Church of Ireland.[12] A curate was indeed often at the mercy of the person who held the advowson of a benefice. The archdeacon of Armagh, Lucas Ussher, was also dependent upon the impropriators,[13] whom, it was reported, usually failed to provide him with any money towards his upkeep.[14] Furthermore, in Armagh it was reported that 'the Approprietoryes have all tythes small and greate And the curates only Easter offerings and psonall dutyes of Marriages, Christenings and buryalls'.[15] This meant that the curate's sole source of income lay in delivering sacraments, and if he did not deliver them in a way which was acceptable to his Catholic parishioners, his income would suffer accordingly as locals looked elsewhere for a clergyman who would use rites of which they approved. The Church of Ireland bishop of Derry, George Downham, reported that some Catholic clergy 'doe for smale rewards divorse marryed couples, and sett them at liberty to mary others, insomuch that there is scarce anie man of yeares but he hath more wyves lyving and fewe women wch have not plurality of husbands'.[16] Malcolm Hamilton, Church of Ireland archbishop of Cashel, and a vehement anti-Catholic, reported in the late 1620s the many charges which he claimed Catholic clergy placed upon their congregation, including a blessing used at baptism without which a man could not later conceive. All of these charges led, Hamilton claimed, to Jesuits and friars leading very comfortable lives.[17] But it was felt by many, including Richard Hadsor, one of the 1622 commissioners and the probable author of a tract on Ireland in 1623 entitled *Advertisements for Ireland*, that the Church of Ireland clerics charged excessively for the administration of sacraments – indeed, in some cases, they exacted both the English dues as well as the traditional Irish duties, a doubly unfair form of extortion.[18] A further petition on behalf of the subjects of Ireland in 1628 also detailed the extortionate attempts of the Protestant clergy, charging '13s. 4d., 10s. and 6s. 8d. respectively for every christening, marriage and funeral', and imprisoning those who failed to pay.[19]

As a result of these impropriations, some buildings associated with the churches were also in the control of the laity. Nowhere was the problem of church impropriations more clearly illustrated than in Dundalk, where in 1622 it was reported that the vicarage had been leased for 100 years at 20s. per annum, forcing the incumbent there to 'hire a house'.[20] James Spottiswood, bishop of Clogher, was forced to live in a rented house, as was the dean of the diocese of Derry.[21] Generally, however, as a result of the Ulster Plantation, impropriations were not as high in Ulster as elsewhere in the country, but on average, 60% of Ireland's parishes were impropriate.[22] Bishop William Bedell of Kilmore even went to the extreme of taking a lawsuit against the widow of his predecessor, Thomas Moyne, in his quest to return to the Church what had been leased away.[23] And three weeks before the death of King James in 1625, Ulster bishops had complained that much of the maintenance of their clergy had been leased away.[24] The problems associated with the short-sighted policy of large-scale leasing and selling of monastic lands and advowsons begun in the 1530s during the

Dr James Spottiswood, bishop of Clogher,
courtesy of Clogher Cathedral

monastic dissolutions had come home to roost by the early seventeenth century.[25]

The physical fabric of the church was a great cause of concern and many churches were in extreme disrepair, in such poor shape it is no wonder that people were not inclined to attend them. It was reported in 1622 that 'The cathedral church of St Columb of derry hath not soe much as any ruines left neither is there any other cathedral or p'ishe church built in steade thereof within the citty of Londonderry'.[26] And in Raphoe in the same year, the clergy complained that 'the ancient parish churches of the said Diocese, were for the most part ruinated, and none of them in good and sufficient repair, and the Parishioners unwilling … to re-edify the same'.[27] The dilapidated state of many of Ireland's churches was not a new problem and had been noted by the privy council in the 1560s.[28] By 1600, Queen Elizabeth was informed that 'the moste parte of Churches within the two large dioceses of Dublin and Meath are utterly ruined in so much as, between Dublin and Athlone … there are so few Churches standing as they will scarcely make a plural number, and so few pastors to teache or preach the word, as in the moste of them there is not soo much as a reading minister'.[29] This state of affairs was a possible result of the Nine Years' War which was raging at this time, but it is also an indication of how little investment lay people were willing to make in their local churches.[30] Some of the damage was even earlier, however, and the cathedral at Armagh was described in 1622 as being 'ruinated', with its steeple having been thrown down by Shane O'Neill, probably in the 1560s.[31] That these churches were never repaired in the meantime points to an unwillingness on the part of the local populace to fund their repair, which implies an unhappiness with the new State Church.[32] As a result, without a local laity willing to repair, rebuild and re-edify their churches, the Church of Ireland clergy were often forced to serve in ruins and shacks.

It is obvious from the 1622 visitation that some attempt at town planning which included the Church of Ireland church as its focal point was now coming into play, particularly in Ulster. Many Ulster plantation towns to this day locate their Church of Ireland church in a central position, often on, or close to its 'diamond'. Churches which lay in the countryside away from the 'civilising' influence of towns were not favoured. It was decided in Raphoe in 1622, that as the old church in Conwall parish was ruined and in a remote place, a new church should instead be built in Letterkenny, which, it was reported, had eighty British families.[33] This despite the fact that the vicar of Conwall was Dougall Campbell, an Irish speaker, who seems to have been well liked by the local Irish population. Now he and his church were to be moved away from the native Irish population who were not, under the terms of the Ulster plantation, supposed to live within the towns. This failure of the Church of Ireland to engage with the Catholics of Ireland was a severe retardant in its spread at this time. The practice of rebuilding a parish church within the new plantation towns for the use of the Church of Ireland population there was not uncommon, and similar cases were reported in the plantation settlements of Belturbet, Virginia and Ballyhaise, County Cavan, in 1622.[34] The notion of a centralised church location was further rationalised in the later 1620s, by which time plantation settlements were becoming more permanent in nature.[35] The building of a church was not a plantation requirement for the undertakers in Ulster, and it has been estimated that only twenty or so new churches were built by those heading the local plantations.[36] Nevertheless, the onus to do so was placed squarely on the shoulders of the undertakers, and their failure to comply with this expectation sometimes caused controversy. In Belturbet, the planters complained in 1622 that there was no church in the town, despite the 'greate store of Protestants [including a minister] in and about the towne' and it was felt that 'there should be a church builded there'.[37] Likewise, in Ardstraw in Tyrone that same year, Sir Robert Newcomen had yet to build the new church which was expected by his planters.[38] Some churches, however, such as that projected at Virginia, were not built until after the Cromwellian Restoration of 1653.[39]

That a Catholic church pledging its allegiance to Rome existed alongside the established Church of Ireland was a fact of life which could not be ignored. Bishop Moyne of Kilmore, in a frank statement from 1622, admitted that as well as his own clergy, jurisdiction was also exercised by a number of

Gaelic Irish clergy 'established by the popes authoritie'.[40] It was also reported that same year by the bishop of Derry, George Downham, that Eugene McMahon, 'pretended archbishop of Dublin, and David Roth, pretended vice primate of Ardmagh usurped jurisdiction within the diocese of Derry by authority from Rome … priests [are] placed in every parish to celebrate mass and exercise other priestly functions, ignorant and vicious fellows that draw after them ignorant people'.[41] The seriousness of this particular point is evidenced by the fact that the thrust of Downham's claim was repeated in the commissioners' final report, which did not usually deal in specifics.[42] This Catholic resurgence in the first half of the seventeenth century has been examined most recently by Brian Mac Cuarta, who points to Continentally-trained Catholic clergy, the failure of Protestant clergy to engage with the Irish Catholics and improved Catholic infrastructure as reasons for the Church of Ireland's failure to impose itself upon the general populace.[43]

This was a problem which the Church of Ireland attempted to counteract through the conversion of Catholic Gaelic Irish clergy to the Protestant faith, but the attempts were often half-hearted. There were some limited successes in converting Gaelic Irish clergy to the Protestant faith, such as Fferall McCabe of Ardagh and Thomas Brady, Shane O Goron and Nicholas Smith of Kilmore, as well as Brian O'Doweny and Owen O'Mullock of Raphoe,[44] but these triumphs were sometimes short lived. One such example was a priest based in Kilmore by the name of Hugh McConnyne, who had converted, but who had been 'suspended [by 1622] for misdemeanours', having lapsed back into the Catholic faith; another was Hugh (Eugene) Maguire, who was educated at Trinity College Dublin as a Protestant minister, only to defect to Catholicism, becoming dean of Clogher by 1628.[45] Even those native Irish clergy who remained within the fold of the Church of Ireland often had Catholic wives and children, much to the exasperation of church leaders.[46] And in one notorious case from the late 1630s, Murtagh King, a Cavan-based cleric who had turned from the Catholic faith to the Church of Ireland, and who aided Bishop William Bedell in his translation of the Old Testament, was accused by Bishop John Bramhall of Derry of harbouring a Catholic wife. Bedell later admitted that she was indeed a Catholic, but claimed that King's 'wife at the tyme when I conferred the living upon him came to Church in my view sundry weekes; now is revolted and his greatest crosse; so unreasonable a woman, as I have often thought her possessed by a wicked spirit and set on by Sathan, to vexe him and disgrace his person'.[47]

Nor were the clergy or commissioners blind to the difficulties of preaching to the Gaelic Irish in a foreign tongue. The lately established Trinity College in Dublin had not produced any meaningful numbers of native clergy capable of preaching in Irish, and Gaelic versions of the New Testament and Book of Common Prayer were not published until 1603 and 1608 respectively, making the celebration of the Protestant service in Ireland a difficult and contentious issue.[48] In a survey of Irish speakers in fourteen dioceses in Ireland during the period 1590–1620, Seán Ó Cearnaigh discovered forty-three Irish readers throughout eight of these dioceses for which there was information extant, an extremely small number.[49] Trinity College had not become the hoped for centre for native Irish clerical students, leading an exasperated King James to issue a sharp reprimand to the college in February 1620. James believed that Trinity College should have at this stage 'good numbers of the natives … trained up and been employed as teachers of the ignorant among the Irish'. That this had not happened, he laid squarely at the feet of the governors of Trinity College, whom the king accused of neglect. The lack of interest which Trinity College had in native Irish clerics was painfully apparent to all observers.[50]

To circumvent this attitude and its related problems, William Andrewes of the parish of Annagh in Kilmore paid £10 yearly to an 'Irish curate to reade divine service in the Irish tongue', as did William Newcomen of Diserttegny in the diocese of Derry, and William Moore of Mahareclowny in Clogher, although not resident himself, kept an Irish vicar.[51] Hugh Griffin in Armagh read the Irish service book himself and in 1622 in the diocese of Derry, it was reported that an Irish man named Patrick McTally, 'having a Little Lattene and no Englishe, but thought by my predecessor sufficient for a parish consisting wholly of Irish', was serving in a parish there. This entry does imply that the bishop there was not happy with this arrangement, but with nothing better available to him, had to accept the situation as it was handed down to him, which was, in his opinion, so full of flaws.[52] The commission recognised the bishops' difficulty here and recommended in their report that they were to 'take special care that the New Testament and Book of Common Prayer which is translated into the Irish tongue be carefully kept and frequently used in the several parishes of the Irishry'.[53] Furthermore, in Raphoe, a number of Protestant clerics employed Irish-speaking curates to serve the native congregation. That they employed these Gaelic Irish clerics implies that they must have had some success in attracting the native Irish to services, otherwise they would not waste the money on an Irish-speaking curate preaching to an empty church.[54] Examples such as these, however, were few. When James VI succeeded to the English throne as James I in 1603, he inherited over half a dozen Irish-speaking bishops. But few of his appointees, mostly Anglophone English and Scots, bothered to learn the language and when he died in 1625, only one of Ireland's bishops was of Gaelic Irish stock. This situation worsened under Charles I, who tended to appoint Church of England clergy personally known to him to Irish bishoprics, further depleting the stock of Irish-speaking bishops.[55]

The English view of the stubborn nature of the Gaelic Irish in resisting the religious reforms was commented upon by more than one observer of Irish affairs at this time and it was felt by some that it was the fault of the Gaelic Irish that they were not accepting the religious reforms. In 1622, Downham of Derry made the following remark as part of his return: 'The incumbent is not resident, but liveth in another diocese repayring sometimes to his cure wch in his absence (if any of his parishners would come as I suppose few or ane doe) would be discarged (after a sort) by his clerke being an Irish scholler'.[56] In essence, the bishop was saying that there was no point in having a resident vicar, as no Gaelic Irish would attend the service anyway. But it is true that the Protestant clergy tended to focus upon the planter community rather than the native Irish one. As already mentioned, Letterkenny was to receive a new church in 1622 for its British families to the exclusion of the native Irish. And the presumably recusant people of Tyrone also complained in 1622 of the imposition of fines of 9d. for failure to attend service. In their defence, they claimed that there were not many churches fit to attend, the implication being, that if the churches were there, they would attend.[57] As Aidan Clarke has noted, 'no systematic effort to arrange for the reception of Catholics was made, and the Church's considerable intellectual energies were directed towards Protestant theological controversy rather than towards debate with Catholics'.[58]

By 1622, it has been estimated that roughly 40,000 recusants in Ireland were either under threat of excommunication or facing arrest for the non-payment of these recusancy fines. Of course, it can be argued that the fines were not always collected nor were the excommunications carried out – indeed it has recently been estimated that during this period, conformity fell by up to 90% and recusancy fines fell to about £500 per annum. Ireland became at this time what has recently been described as a 'haven of popery' for British Catholics fleeing from harsher and more tightly enforced anti-recusancy laws in England, Scotland and Wales.[59] Nevertheless, the threat of fines hung over the heads of those charged with recusancy like Damocles' sword.[60] This threat was carried out in Ulster, as Kilmore cathedral was reported in 1622 as having been 'newly built and repaired' by Bishop Thomas Moyne with £175 in recusancy fines from the archbishop of Armagh – it is unclear, however, whether these fines were raised solely in Kilmore or from the whole country.[61] Lord Balfour built a new church and school in Lisnaskea, County Fermanagh, with money raised from recusants' fines from Cavan and Fermanagh, which demonstrates that not all of the money needed to have been raised in the immediate county.[62] Nevertheless, the numerous clashes which Bishop William Bedell of Kilmore later experienced with Alan Cooke, the chancellor of Kilmore, over what the bishop saw as the unfair imposition of recusancy fines on Catholics in Kilmore, suggests that at least some of the

Bishop William Bedell

money could have originated in the diocese. Despite the cathedral renovations reported in 1622, Bedell still bemoaned its poor condition not long after his arrival there in 1629, stating that it was 'without steeple, bell or font', which leads one to wonder just how extensive the repairs noted in 1622 were or indeed how much Bedell was exaggerating the dilapidation of his new cathedral.[63]

The associated problems of pluralism and absenteeism was a very real one throughout Ireland in the early seventeenth century, the usual justification being that the income derived from one of these livings on its own was not sufficient to support a competent minister. Some also claimed to fear for their safety as British and Protestant clerics in what had been Gaelic areas in Ireland, a point which one of the 1622 commissioners, Sir William Parsons, backed up, claiming that 'having neither congregation, society, or safe abiding, no man of learning would reside'.[64] And in the diocese of Derry in 1622, the clergy there set out an additional three reasons as to why they were not always resident:

1. They are unable to build such houses as they dare dwell.
2. because the country is not as yet so well settled.
3. because they have no state in theire glebes assured unto them by anie legall conveyance.[65]

So neither did the clergy of Derry diocese feel that they had any strong legal claims to their landholdings. The isolated position of the diocese in the most northern part of Ireland was another probable reason for the absenteeism of clergy. Nor did Trinity College governors, who held seven advowsons in neighbouring Raphoe, make any great effort to place their graduates in the benefices in their care, further indication of disinterest in such remote and poor livings.[66]

Pluralism and absenteeism was a widespread problem, yet it was generally agreed that this was a necessary evil given the poverty of the Church of Ireland. But the large unwieldy parishes of Gaelic Ireland often made the policy of pluralism a self-defeating one, a fact to which the commissioners admitted in their report on the church, stating that 'the parsons and vicars presentative are enforced for want of means to supply several cures, whereby they are all the worse served'.[67] Not all bishops, however, agreed with the practice of pluralism in Ireland's parishes. When William Bedell assumed the united bishoprics of Kilmore and Ardagh in 1629, he ridded himself of Ardagh in 1632. Bedell did this, he claimed, as he 'was loth myne owne example should serve for a pretext to the detestable practice of many of our own nation'.[68] But this stance merely served to further antagonise the Church of Ireland clergy of Kilmore and the difficulties which Bedell experienced in his attempts to prevent one of his clerics, John Bayly, from collecting a number of benefices to himself, illustrate the tacit support which the Church of Ireland gave to the practice of pluralism.[69] But in Raphoe, despite the will to grant clergy more than one benefice, they often could not, as the advowsons were held by 'divers Patrons, who will not possibly agree together', another problem associated with the existence of multiple lay impropriators.[70]

So what came of the royal visitation of the Church of Ireland in 1622? Truth be told, the report had very little immediate effect. The commission recommended that those who held advowsons be compelled through the chancery court to provide a reasonable stipend for those serving the cure. They also wished to see an end to pluralism, except if he was a bachelor or doctor of divinity. Even in those cases, the benefices could be no more than ten miles apart. Churches should be granted twenty acres next to the actual church for the cleric to build a house for himself and furthermore, that the churches should be repaired by the parishioners. A proclamation was also made by the lord deputy and the council in January 1624, banishing Catholic priests from Ireland within forty days. The poor state of the physical fabric of the church was commented upon by the commissioners, who advised the king to force parishioners who had entered into bonds to repair and rebuild their local churches to actually do so.[71] The lack of enthusiasm on the part of the Anglican Church to convert the Gaelic Irish was noted by the commissioners, who claimed that if only Anglican clergy in Ulster would carry out their duties efficiently, 'in a short time their churches which are now empty would be filled with auditors'.[72] Of course, making all of these recommendations and proclamations was fine in itself, but there is little or no evidence that anything actually changed as a result.[73]

Indeed, one of the only tangible results of the visitation that could be seen immediately were the demands from Robert Hamilton, rector of Killichill in Armagh. In August 1622, Hamilton complained that his parish had lost a chapel as the result of the commission, which had, according to the irate cleric, wrongly assigned it elsewhere. Accordingly, Hamilton requested that an inquisition be held in order to re-establish Killichill's right to the chapel and its appurtenances.[74] So one of the only immediate effects of the 1622 royal visitation was to attract the ire of an obscure Armagh rector and his parishioners.

But when examined in detail, the 1622 royal visitation of the Church of Ireland reveals the existence of a multitude of problems. Lay impropriation on a massive scale had drastically weakened the physical and financial fabric of the Church of Ireland. Churches and associated buildings were often in ruins with no will on the part of the local population to remedy the problem. The poverty of the benefices meant that there was a difficulty in attracting suitable educated clergy to poorer positions throughout Ireland. Instead, these positions sometimes attracted unwholesome clergy who did not reach the standards expected in England. The negativity displayed towards the native and Old English Catholic community and the failure to engage with them upon a theological level meant that opportunities to win them over were lost. The recusancy fines and unfairly high fees for sacraments charged by some rapacious ministers also turned the Catholic community against the Church of Ireland. The returns for the 1622 royal visitation of the Church of Ireland afford us a view of these weaknesses, problems and squandered opportunities.

Notes

1   Printed in Victor Treadwell (ed.), *The Irish commission of 1622: an investigation of the Irish administration 1615–22 and its consequences 1623–24* (Dublin, 2006), pp 283–99.

2   Normally a side chapel in a church maintained to say Masses for the soul(s) of the deceased benefactor(s).

3   John McCafferty, *The reconstruction of the Church of Ireland: Bishop Bramhall and the Laudian reforms, 1633–1641*(Cambridge, 2007), p. 24; Hugh Kearney, *Strafford in Ireland 1633–41: a study in absolutism* (2nd ed., Cambridge, 1989), ch. 10; Aidan Clarke, 'Varieties of uniformity: the first century of the Church of Ireland' in W.J. Shiels and Diana Wood (eds), *The churches, Ireland and the Irish* (Oxford, 1989), pp 105–22 at pp 120–21; Phil Kilroy, 'Radical religion in Ireland, 1641–1660' in Jane H. Ohlmeyer (ed.), *Ireland: From independence to occupation* (Cambridge, 1995), pp 201–217 at p. 201.

4   P.B. Phair, 'Seventeenth-century regal visitations' in *Analecta Hibernica*, 28 (1978), pp 79–100 at p. 83.

5   Joseph McLaughlin, 'The making of the Irish Leviathan, 1603–25: Statebuilding in Ireland during the reign of James VI and I' (unpublished Ph.D. thesis, National University of Ireland, Galway, 1999), p. 125; Treadwell (ed.), *The Irish commission of 1622*, p. xxix; Raymond Gillespie, *Seventeenth-century Ireland: making Ireland modern* (Dublin, 2006), p. 66; Menna Prestwich, *Cranfield: politics and profits under the early Stuarts* (Oxford, 1966), ch. 8.

6   A more detailed study of the recruitment and membership of the commission can be found in Treadwell (ed.), *The Irish commission of 1622*, pp xxix–xxxvi.

7   Victor Treadwell, *Buckingham and Ireland 1616–1628: a study in Anglo-Irish politics* (Dublin, 1998), p. 198.

8   Treadwell (ed.), *The Irish commission of 1622*, pp lii, 285. The returns for the united dioceses of Meath & Clonmacnoise were published as 'State and revennewes of the Bishoppricke of Meath and Clonmackenosh' in C.R. Elrington (ed.), *The whole works of the most reverend James Ussher* (16 vols, Dublin, 1847) XV, pp liii–cxxv.

9   Treadwell (ed.), *The Irish commission of 1622*, pp xxx–xxxi.

10 The right to appoint a clergyman to a parish or other ecclesiastical benefice.

11 S.G. Ellis, 'Economic problems of the church: why the reformation failed in Ireland' in *Journal of Ecclesiastical History*, 41 (1990), pp 239–65.

12 Treadwell (ed.), *The Irish commission of 1622*, p. xxxi.

13 Those to whom the advowson had been granted.

14 TCD, MS 550, ff 26–27, 160–61.

15 Ibid., f. 44.

16 TCD, MS 550, f. 190. Marriage conventions in Gaelic Ireland were very different from those of the English state, which perhaps accounts for the incredulous tone of this report: Kenneth Nicholls, *Gaelic and Gaelicized Ireland in the Middle Ages* (Dublin, 1973; rpr. 2003), pp 83–7; Gillian Kenny, *Anglo-Irish and Gaelic women in Ireland, c. 1170–1540* (Dublin, 2007), chs 7, 11, 12, 14; Art Cosgrove, 'Marriage in medieval Ireland' in Art Cosgrove (ed.), *Marriage in Ireland* (Dublin, 1985), pp 25–50.

17 Alan Ford, 'Criticising the Godly prince: Malcolm Hamilton's *Passages and consultations*' in Vincent Carey & Ute Lotz-Heumann (eds), *Taking sides? Colonial and confessional Mentalités in early modern Ireland* (Dublin, 2003), pp 116–37 at pp 129–30.

18 George O'Brien (ed.), *Advertisements for Ireland, being a description of Ireland in the reign of James I* (Dublin, 1923); Alan Ford, *The Protestant Reformation in Ireland, 1590–1641* (Dublin, 1997), p. 149.

19 *Cal. S.P. Ire., 1625–32*, pp 337–8; Colm Lennon & Ciaran Diamond, 'The ministry of the Church of Ireland, 1536–1636' in T.C. Barnard & W.G. Neely (eds), *The clergy of the Church of Ireland, 1000–2000: messengers, watchmen and stewards* (Dublin, 2006), pp 44–58 at p. 55.

20 TCD, MS 550, ff 40–41.

21 Armagh Pub. Lib., MS E192, f. 31v; TCD, MS 550, f. 189.

22 Gillespie, *Seventeenth-century Ireland*, p. 67; Ford, *The Protestant Reformation in Ireland*, p. 68.

23 Brendan Scott, *Cavan, 1609–1653: plantation, war and religion* (Dublin, 2007), pp 24–25.

24 McCafferty, *The reconstruction of the Church of Ireland*, p. 25.

25   Brendan Bradshaw, *The dissolution of the religious orders in Ireland under Henry VIII* (Cambridge, 1974), pp 231–47.

26   TCD, MS 550, f. 188.

27   Ibid., ff 226–29.

28   TNA, SP 63/17/8.

29   T.N.A., SP 63/139/47.

30   Steven G. Ellis, *Ireland in the age of the Tudors 1447–1603: English expansion and the end of Gaelic rule* (London & New York, 1998), p. 347; James Murray, *Enforcing the English reformation in Ireland: clerical resistance and political conflict in the diocese of Dublin, 1534–1590* (Cambridge, 2009), pp 60–61.

31   TCD, MS 550, f. 27.

32   Alan Ford believes that the earlier Church visitation of 1615 fails to convey the true extent of church dilapidation in Ireland, whose physical fabric had been allowed by and large to deteriorate unchecked throughout the sixteenth and seventeenth centuries: Ford, *The Protestant reformation in Ireland*, pp 103–05.

33   TCD, MS 550, f. 215.

34   Scott, *Cavan, 1609–1653*, pp 23–4.

35   Annaleigh Margey, 'After the flight: the impact of plantation on the Ulster landscape' in David Finnegan, Éamonn Ó Ciardha & Marie-Claire Peters (eds), *The Flight of the Earls: Imeacht na nIarlaí* (Derry, 2010), pp 246–58 at pp 254–7; eadem, 'Surveying and mapping plantation in Cavan, c. 1580–1622' in Brendan Scott (ed.), *Culture and society in early modern Breifne/Cavan* (Dublin, 2009), pp 106–20 at p. 119.

36   P. Robinson, *The Plantation of Ulster: British Settlement in an Irish Landscape, 1600–1670* (Dublin, 1984; rpr. Belfast, 2000), p. 144.

37   Brendan Scott, 'The 1641 rising in the plantation town of Belturbet' in *Breifne*, 40 (2004), pp 155–75 at pp 161–62; R.J. Hunter, 'Towns in the Ulster Plantation' in *Studia Hibernica*, xi (1971), pp 40–79 at p. 75.

38   TCD, MS 550, f. 194.

39   Robert Hunter, 'The Bible and the bawn: an Ulster planter inventorised' in Ciaran Brady and Jane Ohlmeyer (eds), *British interventions in early modern Ireland* (Cambridge, 2005), pp 116–34 at p. 120; idem, 'An Ulster Plantation town – Virginia' in *Breifne*, 13 (1970), pp 43–51.

40   TCD, MS 550, f. 206.

41   Treadwell (ed.), *The Irish commission of 1622*, p. 293.

42   Ibid., p. 714.

43   Brian Mac Cuarta, *Catholic revival in the north of Ireland, 1603–41* (Dublin, 2007), pp 241–4.

44   TCD, MS 550, ff 146, 148, 156, 212–22; Alan Ford, 'The reformation in Kilmore before 1641' in Raymond Gillespie (ed.), *Cavan: essays on the history of an Irish county* (Dublin, 1995; rpr. 2004), pp 73–98 at p. 97.

45   TCD, MS 550, f. 144; Ford, *The Protestant reformation in Ireland*, p. 146.

46   As did some bishops, notably Roland Lynch of Clonfert and Kilmacduagh and Miler Magrath of Cashel and Emly: Ford, *The Protestant reformation in Ireland*, p. 45.

47   E.S. Shuckburgh (ed.), *Two biographies of William Bedell, bishop of Kilmore* (Cambridge, 1902), p. 342; Brendan Scott, 'The matters objected against Murtagh King, 1638' in *Archivium Hibernicum*, 65 (2012), pp 76–81.

48   Mícheál Mac Craith, 'The Gaelic reaction to the reformation' in Steven G. Ellis & Sarah Barber (eds), *Conquest and union: fashioning a British state, 1485–1725* (London & New York, 1995), pp 139–61 at p. 148.

49   Seán Ó Cearnaigh, 'An Ghaeilge I gcló, 1571–1882' (unpublished Ph.D. thesis, Trinity College Dublin, 1990), p. 65.

50   *Cal. S.P. Ire., 1615–25*, pp 276–7.

51   TCD, MS 550, ff 144–45, 184–5, 191.

52   TCD, MS 550, f. 191. This situation was rectified to the bishop's satisfaction by 1624, when he replaced McTally with one George Perinchief: Ford, *The Protestant reformation in Ireland*, p. 144, fn. 79.

53   Treadwell (ed.), *The Irish commission of 1622*, p. 295.

54   TCD, MS 550, ff 212–29.

55   John McCafferty, 'Protestant prelates or godly pastors? The dilemma of the early Stuart episcopate' in Alan Ford & John McCafferty (eds), *The origins of sectarianism in early modern Ireland* (Cambridge, 2005), pp 54–72 at p. 57; Alan Ford, '"That Bugbear Arminianism": Archbishop Laud and Trinity College, Dublin' in Brady & Ohlmeyer (eds), *British interventions in early modern Ireland*, p. 139, fn. 18.

56   TCD, MS 550, f. 202.

57   McCafferty, *The reconstruction of the Church of Ireland*, pp 147, 149–50.

58   Clarke, 'Varieties of Uniformity', p. 119.

59   David Edwards, 'A haven of popery: English Catholic migration to Ireland in the age of plantations' in Ford & McCafferty (eds), *The origins of sectarianism in early modern Ireland*, pp 95–126.

60   Treadwell, *Buckingham and Ireland 1616–1628*, pp 220–23.

61   TCD, MS 550, ff 142–3; Scott, *Cavan, 1609–1653*, p. 23. The church at Urney in Derry diocese was also earmarked for repairs with the help of recusancy fines from the archbishop of Armagh in 1622: TCD, MS 550, f. 193.

62   Robinson, *The plantation of Ulster*, pp 144–5.

63   Shuckburgh (ed.), *Two biographies of William Bedell*, p. 300; Scott, *Cavan, 1609–1653*, pp 26–7.

64   Quoted in Ford, *The Protestant Reformation in Ireland*, p. 148.

65   TCD, MS 550, f. 189.

66   Ford, *The Protestant reformation in Ireland*, p. 142.

67   Treadwell (ed.), *The Irish commission of 1622*, p. 285.

68   Shuckburgh (ed.), *Two biographies of William Bedell*, p. xvii.

69   Scott, *Cavan, 1609–1653*, p. 26.

70   TCD, MS 550, f. 222.

71   Treadwell (ed.), *The Irish commission of 1622*, p. 290.

72   Ibid., p. 286.

73   Treadwell (ed.), *The Irish commission of 1622*, pp 709–16; McCafferty, *The reconstruction of the Church of Ireland*, p. 24.

74   Treadwell (ed.), *The Irish commission of 1622*, p. 302.

The 1641 depositions:
a window on life and society
in seventeenth-century Ulster

Elaine Murphy[1]

On 31 December 1641, Richard Morse, the rector of Inishmacsaint parish in County Fermanagh, gave a deposition in which he outlined the attack on his family and property at the outbreak of the 1641 rebellion in late October of that year. In his deposition, Morse gave a very harrowing account of the journey his family made as they fled from the rebellion. He described how the insurgents:

> did in a most barbarous, cruell, & inhumane manner, stripp this deponent out of all his Apparell naked, and in lyke manner vsed his wyfe and six small Children & two seruants, leauing some of them only their smocks, and some peeces of Raggs, which hardly could couer their shame, and at that tyme did beat & wound this deponent & were lyke to haue murdred him.

Only Morse, his wife and two of the children reached safety in Dublin. One child died on the road and 'three others being therby lame & sick & not able to trauell are left behind in the said County of Cauan to the mercy of the Enemye and knoweth not what is become of them'.[2] Morse's deposition demonstrates some of the horrors of the 1641 rebellion in Ulster as Protestants fled across the country, in the depths of winter, to try to save their lives. As well as showing the barbarity of the rising, however, Morse's deposition is also a treasure trove of information about a variety of aspects of life in seventeenth-century Ulster. In it, he provided details and values for the crops, livestock and household goods stolen by the rebels. His deposition included a list of leases that he held and debts due to him from people in the county. Morse also furnished very precise evidence about the rebels who assaulted his family. He named the specific insurgents and

At one M.ʳ Atkins house & Papistes brake in & beate out his braines, then riped upe his wife with Childe, after they had rauished her, & Nero like vewed natures bed of conception then tooke they the Childe & sacrificed it in the fire.

Engraving from the *Teares of Ireland*, 1642

provided their addresses and any other personal information he knew about them. Despite the richness of the information contained within the Ulster depositions, however, much of the focus of historical research on the province has been on the causes of the rebellion or the atrocities which took place.[3] In looking at the historiography of the 1641 depositions Aidan Clarke noted that they have been 'continuously evoked … but they were rarely opened in the process'.[4] Therefore, this essay seeks to showcase the potential of the 1641 depositions as a source for the study of early modern Ulster.

The 1641 depositions are a collection of over 8,000 witness statements housed in the Old Library of Trinity College Dublin.[5] John Sterne, the bishop of Clogher, gifted the depositions to Trinity College in 1741 to mark the centenary of the rising. Every county in Ireland is represented in thirty-three manuscript volumes of depositions. The depositions are made up of thirty-one volumes (MSS 809–839) covering each county, a miscellaneous volume of papers relating to the rebellion (MS 840) and an index volume (MS 841). They are currently divided on a county-by-county basis with eleven volumes from Leinster, ten from Munster, eight relating to Ulster and two from Connacht. The number of depositions varies considerably for each county. In Ulster, for example, there are sixty-four

English Protestantes striped naked & turned into the mountaines, in the frost, & snowe, whereof many hundreds are perished to death, & many liynge dead in diches & Sauages upbraided them saynge now are ye wilde Irish as well as wee.

Engraving from the *Teares of Ireland*, 1642

pages of surviving depositions for County Donegal and sixty-two pages for County Londonderry, both contained in MS 839. By way of contrast the depositions for County Cork take up over 3,900 pages and six and a half volumes (MSS 822–828). They are one of the most important sources of information about the outbreak and spread of the 1641 rebellion in Ireland and its aftermath. They are also an important source of information on economic, political and social aspects of life in Ireland including agricultural activity, industrial activity, overseas trade, religious practice, military campaigning and social customs among many others.

The Ulster depositions in print

The 1641 depositions, especially those from Ulster, have had a troubled historiography.[6] Selections from the depositions began to appear in print as early as 1642 and continued to be published in the decades and centuries that followed. Henry Jones, the head of the depositions commission, printed a large number of excerpts relating to the province in two publications. In *A Remonstrance of Divers Remarkeable Passages Concerning the Church and Kingdom of Ireland*, published in London in 1642, fifty-two of the seventy-eight exemplar testimonies selected by Jones came from Ulster.[7] Sir John Temple's *The Irish Rebellion*, first published in 1646, also made extensive use of Ulster depositions and was reprinted through the seventeenth, eighteenth and nineteenth centuries in times of political and religious crisis.[8] These early editions removed more of the mundane material contained within the testimonies, such as the details of financial losses. Instead, they tended to concentrate on more controversial and sensational elements of the evidence to elicit sympathy and relief in England for the dispossessed Protestants in Ireland. For example, Margaret Parkin in County Fermanagh recounted information about the losses she suffered, being stripped naked by the rebels and the death of her husband *en route* to the siege of Drogheda. Parkin also reported that she heard 'the Rebels boyled a younge Childe to death in a Caldron or great Kettle in the Church at Newtowne'. The extract of her deposition printed in the *Remonstrance* made no mention of the other information she gave and instead focused on the story of the murder of the child.[9]

Reprinting the depositions remained divisive into the nineteenth and twentieth centuries in Ireland. Mary Hickson's *Ireland in the Seventeenth Century*, published in 1884, was the first book to print a substantial number of depositions in nearly 250 years. Hickson's work, however, perpetuated the Protestant version of 1641 and discredited contemporary Irish Catholics' calls for political and land reform. Unsurprisingly, Hickson's account of the depositions prompted vigorous rebuttals of her conclusions from a Catholic perspective, as exemplified by Thomas Fitzpatrick's *Bloody Bridge*.[10] This tit-for-tat exchange of denial and counter-denial lasted until the 1960s.[11] Attempts to publish the depositions in the 1930s and 1960s came to nothing as the Irish government feared exacerbating tensions north and south of the border.[12] Difficulties of access to and the ability of scholars to read the depositions served to limit much of the historical scholarship that has been undertaken on the Ulster depositions. Research on the province tended to concentrate on the outbreak of the rebellion and events connected with it in the province, the numbers of people killed there and regional studies of counties.[13] The online publication of the depositions opens up a whole new range of research possibilities into early modern Ulster.[14]

The 1641 Rebellion and the depositions

On the evening of 22 October 1641 Owen Connolly, a servant to Sir John Clotworthy, revealed to government officials in the city the details of a plot by some Ulstermen to seize Dublin Castle. Connolly claimed to have learned the details of the plot while drinking with Hugh Óg McMahon, his foster brother and one of the principal conspirators.[15] The lords justices in Dublin acted promptly to prevent the attack on the castle by closing the city gates and arresting the leading plotters, including McMahon and Lord

Margaret Parkin of Newtowne in the Countie of
Fermanagh widowe duly sworne deposeth That about
the 23 of october last past at Newtowne aforesaid
the Rebelles beinge a very greate number who surprised &
robbed all the other subiects of the same Towne) came
into the dwelling house and rifled the house and tooke
away all the goods that she and her husband had and
stripped both her and her husband and 3 Children all starke naked and turned them all out
of doores to the other under a hedge and to the value of
about 6 ... her husband was slayne goinge Frydays with the
Company that went to relieve the Towne) And the deponent
further sayth that by the informacon of divers Credible
persons the Rebelles did boyle a yonge Childe to death
in a Caldron or great Kettle in the Church at Newtowne

Jur 19 Jan 1641.

Roger Puttocke

William Aldrich

Margaret Parkin

Conor Maguire, along with anyone else suspected of involvement.[16] In the days and months that followed, many of the prisoners were examined before government officials in Dublin. Torture was used to obtain confessions from some suspects, including Hugh Óg McMahon, whose deposition was 'taken at the rack'.[17] In their examinations, those interrogated outlined or denied their involvement in the plot to seize the city, the reasons behind the rebellion and what they hoped to achieve. The leading plotters did not deny their knowledge or involvement in the rebellion. On 23 October, McMahon stated that 'there wilbee trouble this day throughout all the Kingdome of Ireland, and that all the fortifications of Ireland wilbee this day taken'.[18] Lord Maguire outlined the longer history of the planned rebellion and named other leading conspirators as well as admitting 'that the sayd Castle of Dublin was to haue been surprised by himselfe'.[19] A number of those arrested professed to be innocent of any part in the rebellion and gave various explanations for being in Dublin. William Moore from Monaghan and Tirlagh mc Scholane of Fermanagh claimed to be in the city to enlist with a captain for service in the Spanish army. Edmond O Doghertie from County Down deposed that he went to Dublin as he heard his brother had returned there from England.[20]

The maintenance of the element of surprise allowed the rebel leaders in Ulster to succeed where their co-conspirators in Dublin failed. On 22–3 October, they seized a number of the most important fortifications in the province. Sir Phelim O'Neill captured Charlemont fort under the pretence that he was calling on the governor for dinner.[21] In the days that followed, other key garrisons and towns, including Armagh, Tandragee, Mountjoy Castle, Newry and Dungannon fort also fell to the rebels. As word of the rebellion spread, a number of towns, including Coleraine, Carrickfergus, Derry, and Enniskillen managed to hold out against the insurgents. From the beginning of the rising in Ulster many of the attacks on Protestants in the province were bloody and brutal. For example, on the morning of 23 October 1641, Arthur Champion and at least seven others were killed at Shannock Castle in Fermanagh. One account of the killing noted that the victims were not properly buried and that one corpse lay 'vnburied above ground vntill the doggs had eaten a great part of him'.[22] Many Protestants fled from their homes towards Dublin or other places of safety as their neighbours and other attacked them. The rebellion spread throughout the country and by Christmas 1641 there were reports of trouble in many counties. In December 1641, the Protestant citizens of Limerick city complained that Dominick Fanning, the mayor, robbed them of their goods and used his position to discover the weak defences of King John's Castle.[23] As refugees began to arrive in Dublin it provided an impetus to take statements and gather evidence about what happened and who perpetrated the crimes against them.

The initial commission to gather evidence about the rebellion was issued on 23 December 1641 by the lords justices of Ireland in the name of the king. They appointed eight clergymen, headed by Dr Henry Jones, the dean of Kilmore and after 1645 the bishop of Clogher, as commissioners to examine 'all such persons as have been robbed and dispoiled, as all witnesses that can give testimony therein, what robberies and spoils have been committed upon them since the 22 of October last'.[24]

In the months that followed, the scope and nature of the original commission was widened to allow the commissioners to enquire into other matters including murder, forced conversion of Protestants to Catholicism and 'traiterous or disloyal words' uttered by the insurgents.[25] The lords justices hoped that the establishment of a commission would enable the gathering of evidence to punish the rebels, provide a record to prevent the same thing happening again and provide a means of relief for some of those who had suffered.[26] The bulk of statements taken by the Dublin commission were made in 1642, though the commissioners continued their work until 1647.[27]

The depositions taken by the Dublin-based commissioners are some of the best known and cited items in the collection.[28] But there are a number of other distinct categories of statements contained within the depositions. In 1645 and 1646, Thomas Waring, the clerk of the commission, made fair copies of many of the depositions taken at Dublin.[29] The practical difficulties for Protestants from Munster reaching Dublin led to the establishment of a separate commission for that province. In March 1642, Philip Bysse, an English clergyman, was appointed to take depositions there. Bysse and his assistants collected evidence in the province until July 1643.[30] A final series of depositions were compiled between 1652 and 1654. In September 1652, seventy commissioners were appointed by parliament to examine witnesses, try cases and impose punishment on captured rebels. The nature of these depositions was somewhat different to those taken in the 1640s. In the 1650s the deponents gave evidence about specific incidents or individuals accused of crimes relating to the rebellion rather than details of their own general experience. Many of the examinants in the 1650s were detained in gaols or under indictment for their own participation in the rebellion.[31] There are also a number of miscellaneous items contained within the collection including letters, indices, copies of oaths and recognizances.

The commissions issued in 1641 and 1642 set out the issues for the commissioners to enquire into and depositions taken in the 1640s generally contained the same core elements. They follow a set format in which the deponent states their name and gives their address in some form. Most deponents, and nearly all the women, mention their occupation or social position. Some of the deponents state their age, nationality and religion.[32]

the Lord Blany forced to ride 14.
Miles without Bridle or Sadell to saue
his life; his Lady Lodged in Strawe,
beeing allowed 2ᵈ a day to releue her,
& her Children, slew a kindsman of
hers and hanged him vp before her
face, 2 dayes telling her, she must expect
the same to terrifie her the moore ,,.

Engraving from the *Teares of Ireland*, 1642

The deponents then outline, in varying degrees of detail, the losses they have suffered as a result of the rebellion and identify the rebels who attacked them. They then proceed to relate any other events they experienced or had first hand experience of, such as atrocities they witnessed, conversations they had with insurgents and their escape to Dublin. The deponents also relate any other information they know about the rebellion by second hand means, such as massacres they heard about and the plans of the rebels. The deponents usually described this as 'credibly hearing' or being 'credibly informed' of this information. Charity Chappel, for example, reported that 'she hath credibly heard that the Rebells did murther & kill divers protestant ministers' in County Armagh. In the same county, Ellenor Fullerton was 'credibly informed that the Rebells burned divers protestants in a howse together in or nere the parish of Kilmore'.[33]

The Ulster depositions

The Ulster depositions consist of 1,928 folios in eight volumes of manuscripts (MSS 832–839).[34] Finding out what happened in Ulster is not as simple, however, as looking merely in these volumes; a number of quirks within the depositions mean that it can be easy to overlook other material of relevance and interest. Many statements by people from Ulster or

Mr Dauenant and his Wife bound in their Chaires; Striped the 2 Eldest Children of 7 years old roſted them upon Spittes before their Parents faces, Cutt their throte, and after murdred him.

Engraving from the *Teares of Ireland*, 1642

relating to events there can also be found in the Dublin and miscellaneous volumes. For example, the examinations given by people arrested in connection with the unsuccessful plot to seize Dublin Castle are in MS 809. One deposition from another province, given by Paul Kingston from County Cork, is bound in with an Ulster volume. The county name was mis-read as Louth and it was placed in MS 834 rather than in one of the Cork volumes.[35] Some depositions are misfiled in the wrong county within the province: Jane Beere's examination forms part of the Antrim volume even though she gave her address as County Armagh and deposed extensively about events there.[36] Examinants in the 1650s are often placed within volumes based on where they gave their evidence and not what they depose about. Margaret Kelly, a widow living at Carrickmacross in 1641, gave evidence about the rebellion in County Monaghan. In 1654, when she deposed, she lived in Dundalk in County Louth and is as a result placed with the depositions for that county.[37]

Within Ulster there is a wide variation in the number of depositions per county. County Cavan is made up of two volumes and 527 folios (MSS 832–3) while Counties Derry, Donegal and Tyrone share a small volume of 156 folios (MS 839). County Louth is included in Ulster and forms part of MS 834 with County Monaghan. (See Table 1 for a full breakdown of the depositions for each county).

Table 1: A Breakdown of the Ulster depositions[38]

Volume (County)	No. of Folios	No. of Deponents	Male Deponents	Female Deponents
MS 832 and MS 833 (Cavan)	527	244	192	52 (21%)
MS 834 (Louth/ Monaghan)	204	106	70	36 (34%)
MS 835 (Fermanagh)	266	154	99	56 (35%)
MS 836 (Armagh)	269	134	100	34 (25%)
MS 837 (Down)	189	123	104	19(15%)
MS 838 (Antrim)	317	260	221	39 (15%)
MS 839 (Derry/ Donegal/Tyrone)	156	77	56	21 (27%)
Total	1,928	1,099	843	256 (23.3%)

There is also a wide variation in the different types of deposition that can be found within each county. There are a large number of duplicate depositions contained in many of the Ulster manuscripts. Thomas Waring, the clerk of the commission, copied 335 of the Ulster depositions.[39] The scarcity of depositions for some areas may be partially explained by local circumstances including the ability of local garrisons to withstand the rebel attacks, as at Enniskillen and Londonderry, or access to escape routes from Ulster by sea such as at Ballyshannon. For example, the majority of depositions from Antrim and Down are from the 1650s. In late 1641 and early 1642, many Protestants fleeing the onslaught of the rebellion in these counties found safety in towns that held out against the rebels, such as Carrickfergus, or took shipping to Scotland. Hence very few refugees from these counties made it to Dublin to testify before the commissioners there. In the 1650s, witnesses from these counties came forward to be examined about the rebellion, sometimes on more than one occasion, before high courts of justice. For example, Edward Sanders, a gentleman from Maze in County Down, related his experiences on two occasions in May and June 1653.[40] Many of these examinations relate to a specific person or incident which was under investigation. In Antrim many of the 1650s examinations concerned the massacre perpetrated by the Scots against the Irish at Island Magee in 1642.[41]

The people of Ulster in the depositions

There are 1,099 individual deponents in the Ulster depositions.[42] This breaks down as 843 male deponents and 256 female. Overall 23% of the deponents in the province were women (see Table 1). Relatively few deponents explicitly stated their nationality or religion in the Ulster depositions. Seventy-nine described themselves as English or British Protestants. In reality most of the deponents who swore before the commissioners in the 1640s about their experiences and sufferings must have been Protestant. In the 1650s the situation became more complex as Catholic witnesses gave statements about their own involvement or the involvement of others in the rising. None of these deponents stated that they were Catholic. Nevertheless, many such as Phelim O'Neill, one of the leaders of the rebellion, can be clearly identified as being Catholic. Names alone should not, however, be taken to indicate that a person was Catholic or Protestant. For example Donnogh Conner, a deponent in Wexford, deposed in 1642 that he 'haveing beene formerly a Romish preist, but by the light of gods truth become a protestant'.[43]

A large numbers of depositions also referred to Protestants converting to Catholicism to save their lives or goods. In Cavan, Phillip O Cur, Shane mc Curr and Turloagh mc Caddow 'lost ther religion being Protestants & fell to papistry'.[44] Unsurprisingly, none of those who gave depositions mentioned that this happened to them. Ulster deponents sometimes referred to the religion or ethnicity of other people they mentioned, usually as rebels or victims, in their depositions. Richard Newberry, a gentleman from Loughgall in Armagh, described how two of his servants – 'both irishmen' – joined the rebels. In June 1643, Peter Gates described how 'James ffarrell a papist of Ballykelly' betrayed and murdered his English neighbours.[45] At Kilmore in County Armagh, Jane Hampson 'formerly a protestant, but a meere irish woman & lately turned to Masse' led a party of rebels who burned a group of Protestants to death.[46] Some deponents accused the Scots in the province of joining with the rebels. Christopher Meanes, from County Cavan, described his tenant, 'Archy Ellett a Scotchman', as 'being in open Rebellion'.[47] Others described Scottish victims being robbed and murdered by the insurgents. Ambrose Bedell, in the same county, heard that a 'a poore Scottish boy about 8 or 10 yere old' met with some 'yong rebell irish boys' who killed him by 'throwing him into a bogpitt threw turfe vpon him and held him in the water vntill they had drowned him'.[48] John Abram, deposing about an event in January 1642, described how 'Lewy Og O Haghian & about fifty or sixty Irish men' attacked a house and robbed and stripped the inhabitants before they killed 'John Spratt a Scotch man' and another unnamed man. By the time he gave his evidence, only two of the rebels who attacked the house that night remained alive to be tried.[49]

As well as religion and ethnicity, many deponents gave their age in their deposition. 329 deponents stated their age which ranged from sixteen to ninety years of age. John Kershaw, a linen weaver from Fermanagh, was the oldest deponent who gave his age as ninety-four in January 1642.[50] The oldest female deponent in the province was Jennett Service, aged 80 in 1653, from Ballycastle in County Antrim.[51] Avis Braishawe was the youngest deponent who deposed in 1642, describing herself as 'being an English Protestant, Aged sixteene yeares or thereabouts'.[52] Two examinants, Anne Bull aged seventeen and Jane Armstrong aged sixteen or seventeen, gave depositions in April and May 1653. Both women deposed about events that occurred during their childhood in the initial stages of the rebellion in 1641 and 1642, Bull stating 'That at the begininge of the Rebellion shee was about six yeares of Age'.[53] The ages related by deponents cannot be wholly relied upon, however, and many depositions, including those of Bull and Armstrong, show a lack of precision about dating. A good example of this is provided by the examination of Robert Merryman from County Down. In three separate depositions in April and May 1653, he stated that he was seventy, seventy-two and seventy-five years old.[54] Other than examples such as these, however, the depositions contain very little information about the age of other people in Ulster. A few deponents commented on the age of either the rebels or victims if they were very young or old. Anthony Stratford heard that in Armagh 'many yong children were cutt into quarters and gobetts by the Rebells And that 18 Scottish infants were hanged on a Clothiers tenterhooks And that *they* murthered a yong fatt Scotchman, and made Candles of his grease'.[55] Ellen Adams deposed how a group of rebels led by Rory Maguire 'inhumanely murthered Joseph Berry an ancient adged man, past foure scoure yeres of adge takeing noe Compassion of his weaknes nor gray haires'.[56] The killing of new-born babies and their mothers particularly shocked many deponents. Philip Taylor claimed first-hand knowledge of the killing of a woman pregnant with twins at Newry as rebels 'ript vp her belly she being with chyld of 2 children & threw her & the children into a ditch: and this deponent drive a sowe from away that was eating one of the children'.[57] In Donegal, Anne Dutton accused James McIlbridy of killing William McKenny's pregnant wife and that he 'ript vpp her belly (shee being greate with child), & tooke & cutt the child out of her wambe'.[58]

One of the real strengths of the depositions is the amount of information they contain about people's position in society. Most deponents gave their occupation or some other status indicator. The status or occupation of the deponents included most strata of society in Ulster including nobility, gentry, military men, tradesmen, merchants, farmers, labourers and servants. In particular, the depositions shed light on the position of women in the province. One of the highest ranked deponents in the whole collection is that of Alice, countess dowager of Antrim, who deposed at Coleraine in February 1653. Being extensively examined about her failure to protect Protestants at Ballycastle in Antrim from the rebels, the countess replied that 'shee was no souldier to go out and defend them'.[59] In the case of female deponents they usually expressed their position in relation to a male relative as a wife, widow or daughter or an employer. Anne Bullinbrook from Tyrone deposed that she was 'the Relict of John Bullinbrooke, Master of the ffreeschoole of the Countie, deceased'.[60] From the details they provided some women had clearly been married on more than one occasion. Jennett Service, the oldest female deponent, began her deposition 'Jennett Service als Hunter als Camill aged eighty years the wife of John Campbell'.[61] Whether or not unmarried women, or the commissioners and clerk who recorded their depositions, defined themselves as spinsters, is difficult to ascertain definitively. By the seventeenth-century, the term spinster was being used to define unmarried women, but it could also refer to a woman who spun thread as an occupation.[62] Jane Cutherbertson in County Cavan described herself as 'the wiffe of James Cuthbertson' and a spinster while Elizabeth Northope, a spinster from Monaghan, deposed about the murder of her father-in-law.[63] A number of women in the province used the term 'singlewoman' to define the themselves. Katherin Greame referred to herself as a 'Singlewoman aged 20 yeares or there abouts, & seruant to Mrs Jane Elly of Kilmakeuit, in Com. Antrim'. Joice Kinde from Lisnegarvy also described herself as a singlewoman in her examination in 1653.[64]

The experiences of the rebellion of women who did not depose can also be seen in the depositions. Most Protestant women appear as victims who suffered at the hands of the rebels. Very few cases of rape were reported in the depositions, but some were alluded to in Ulster. Gilbert Pemberton, a gentleman in Dublin, deposed on behalf of his wife's family in Armagh. He claimed that 'he hath credibly heard, his said Neece being a pretty woman they tooke to themselues to keepe and to vse or rather abuse her as a whore'. George Burne, a miller from Tyrone, reported that before the rebels killed a Mr Allen, an English Protestant, they 'first ravished the said Mr Allens Wiffe as before her husbands face'.[65] One Protestant woman was killed for allegedly being a witch. Edmond Oge O'Donelly claimed that he drowned James Maxwell's wife because 'Sir Phelemie o Neile told him that the said mr Maxwells wife was a Witch & that he neuer had good loocke after he once kissed her'.[66] Irish women in Ulster, on the other hand, are almost always portrayed as instigators or encouragers of violence and attacks on Protestants in the depositions. Alice Gregg outlined the details of the massacre of some Protestants at Loughgall church. Those that managed to escape the initial killing spree by the rebels 'were after most cruelly murthered by the very irish criples & these base trulls that kept them company which Creples & *lewd women* did much vawnt & glory in such their crueltes wherein they had noe little assistance by their children'.[67] Marmaduke Batemanson charged Rose ny Neile with being a 'bloudy viragoe' and claimed that she 'was the principall cawser & instigator of the drowning of fifty protestants men, women, and Children, all at one tyme, at the bridge of Belturbett' in County Cavan.[68]

The landscape of Ulster in the depositions

In addition to the information about people in Ulster the depositions are also a major resource for the study of landscape and settlement in the region. In his study of County Cork, Nicholas Canny noted that the depositions were 'more evidently useful for the purpose of understanding the extent, location and character of the English settler presence in Ireland' at the outbreak of the 1641 rebellion.[69] Historical geographers, such as Annaleigh Margey and William Smyth, have examined various changes in the geography of Ulster that can be seen in the 1641 depositions. The establishment and development of towns was a major part of the plantation of the province in the early seventeenth century.[70] Smyth described how the '[1641] depositions point to the fullness and diversity of a maturing English-style community [in Ireland], albeit a community under stress and in much disarray'.[71] The depositions contain a wide range of detail about the make-up and life of urban centres in the northern counties. The physical landscape of towns can be identified in descriptions of churches, houses, market crosses and defences such as bawns and walls. Elizabeth Gormally who lived 'in the Irish quarter neare to the west port of Carrickfergus' made reference to the walls and 'key gate' of the town in her deposition. Captain John MacAdam gave information in 1644 in which he described how soldiers from his regiment marched to Belfast and there 'by like orders from the Generall Major Monroe they had that morning torne in peeces their cullors in the markett place'.[72]

As well as physical characteristics of towns, the depositions include reports on the civic governance within urban centres. Thomas Theaker, the sovereign of Belfast in 1644, outlined the process of electing burgesses for the town in his testimony. In County Armagh, John Parry mentioned the king's charter to the town of Armagh and the sovereign who was displaced by the rebels.[73] A whole range of economic activity can also be seen within Ulster from the depositions. A number of deponents made references to market days in towns, including Carrickmacross, Glaslough and Virginia.[74] Some residents in Ulster clearly made a success of their business enterprises. John Gowrly, a merchant in the town of Armagh, claimed that he lost wares and merchandise in his shop in Armagh valued at £1,000 and a further £200 worth of goods in his shop at Loughgall.[75] The tastes of people in Ulster in consumer goods can be seen in the items listed by William Smith, a Belturbet merchant. Among the items pillaged from him by the insurgents he noted 'wares in the shopp vizt broadcloath kersies frizes hopps Iron steele Stockings Tobacco to the value of CCC li [£300]'.[76] The depositions are thus one of the most important sources for the investigation of urban history in Ulster.

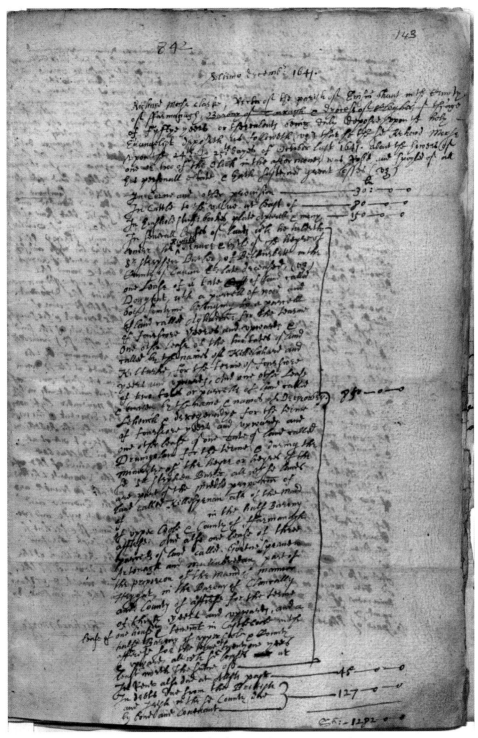

Deposition of Richard Morse, County Fermanagh,
courtesy of the Board of Trinity College Dublin

Rural life in the mid-seventeenth century is one of the most difficult aspects of society to trace from surviving records. The level of detail provided in many depositions about place names as well as people means the depositions offer the potential to survey rural life and settlement in the north of Ireland at parish and in some cases townland level. Within the Ulster volumes, a wide array of aspects of rural settlement and economic activity can be found. These range from the livestock and household goods people owned, the type of landholdings and leases they possessed, the houses they lived in and their interactions with their neighbours. Numerous deponents described the physical characteristics of their houses and out buildings, sometimes specifying if they were stone built. Richard Morse, the deponent whose account opened this article, complained that some rebels occupied stone houses he owned in Fermanagh. In the same county, Martha Slacke, a widow, lost two stone houses left to her by her father.[77] The variety of livestock and crops grown can be seen in Captain Henry Smith's deposition in County Down. Smith detailed the loss of goods worth £913 13s. 4d., including cattle, oxen, sheep and swine which he described as all of 'English breed', different types of poultry, horses, corn, malt, barley, hay, wood, turf, ready money, plate, clothes and household goods.[78] Local interactions within the Ulster counties can also be seen in the way many deponents named people who they rented land to or from and also named those who owed them money in the locality. Arthur Magneiss was owed £8 by Hugh mc Glassney Magneiss and £5 from Daniell o Morgan, both also from County Down, which he believed lost due to the rebellion.[79] John Greg and Richard Warrin, both yeomen from Loughgall in Armagh, leased land and water mills from John Elcock.[80]

Conclusion

Writing in 1986 on the depositions, Aidan Clarke noted the difficulties that abounded in using the collection because of confusion over the way it was arranged. He described how 'no two books have a similar make-up, and this has defeated both sampling and generalization'.[81] Indeed those who examined the depositions were more likely to 'ransack them for ammunition rather than to examine them systematically'.[82] Therefore, the online publication of the depositions offers the potential for researchers, or indeed the curious, to investigate many aspects of life in early-modern Ulster. This article has attempted to provide a taster of some of the potential for further research that can be found in the collection. The depositions offer a wealth of information, largely untapped, about the province, its people and their society. The availability of the full corpus online also highlights the importance of not treating events in Ulster in isolation. The rebellion and its aftermath, as well as characteristics of everyday life in Ulster, can now be compared and contrasted with those elsewhere in Ireland. The similarities and differences in a variety of facets of life can be assessed, such as agricultural practices and livestock values in different parts of the country. For example, Henry Smith in County Down valued his oxen at £3 each in 1642. In other counties the price given by deponents for their oxen varied from £1 14s. to £3 in the same year.[83] Perhaps the best place to conclude is with John Morrill's rallying cry for the 1641 depositions, 'All I am saying is more work is needed'.[84]

Notes

1   I am grateful to Annaleigh Margey for her helpful comments on an earlier draft of this article.

2   All depositions cited in this article are taken from the online edition of the 1641 depositions: https://1641.tcd.ie. Deposition of Richard Morse, 31 Dec. 1641, MS 835, ff 143r–v.

3   Mary Hickson, *Ireland in the Seventeenth Century* (2 vols, London, 1884); Thomas Fitzpatrick, *The Bloody Bridge and other papers Relating to the Insurrection of 1641: Sir Phelim O'Neill's Rebellion* (Dublin, 1903); Nicholas Canny, 'What really happened in Ireland in 1641' in Jane Ohlmeyer (ed.), *Ireland from Independence to Occupation* (Cambridge, 1995), pp 25–42; Brian Mac Cuarta, 'Religious violence against settlers in south Ulster, 1641–2' in Clodagh Tait, David Edwards & Pádraig Lenihan (eds), *Age of atrocity: violence and political conflict in early modern Ireland* (Dublin, 2007), pp 154–75; Joseph Cope, *England and the 1641 Irish Rebellion* (Woodbridge, 2009); David O'Hara, *English Newsbooks and the Irish Rebellion, 1641–1649* (Dublin, 2006).

4   Aidan Clarke, 'The 1641 depositions' in Peter Fox (ed.), *Treasures of the Library, Trinity College Dublin* (Dublin, 1986), pp 111–22 at p. 111

5   The depositions have been available online since October 2010. Details of the project to conserve, digitise and transcribe the depositions can be found on the website.

6   Toby Barnard, '"Parlour entertainment in an evening?" Histories of the 1640s' in Micheál Ó Siochrú (ed.), *Kingdoms in Crisis: Ireland in the 1640s* (Dublin, 2001), pp 20–43; Nicholas Canny, *Making Ireland British, 1580–1650* (Oxford, 2001), pp 461–9; Walter Love, 'Civil War in Ireland: Appearances in Three Centuries of Historical Writing' in *The Emory University Quarterly*, vol. 22, no. 1 (1966), pp 57–72; Clodagh Tait, David Edwards & Pádraig Lenihan, 'Early Modern Ireland: a history of violence' in *Age of Atrocity*, pp 9–33 at pp 12–17.

7   This reflected the fact that the majority of depositions taken by the commissioners between December 1641 and March 1642 came from Ulster. Henry Jones, *A Remonstrance of Divers Remarkeable Passages Concerning the Church and Kingdom of Ireland* (London, 1642), pp 17–81; idem, *An Abstract of Some Few of those Barbarous Cruell Massacres and Murthers of the Protestants and English in Some Parts of Ireland* (London, 1652), pp 7–11; James Cranford's *Teares of Ireland*, published in 1642, also included images of the alleged attacks made upon British settlers: James Cranford, *The teares of Ireland wherein is lively presented as in a map a list of the unheard off cruelties and perfidious treacheries of blood-thirsty Jesuits and the popish* (London, 1642).

8   John Temple, *The Irish rebellion: or, An history of the beginnings and first progresse of the general rebellion raised within the kingdom of Ireland, upon the three and twentieth day of October, in the year, 1641* (London, 1646).

9   Jones, *Remonstrance*, p. 67; deposition of Margaret Parkin, 19 Jan. 1642, MS 835, f. 154r.

10   Hickson, *Ireland in the Seventeenth Century*; Fitzpatrick, *The Bloody Bridge*.

11   Love, 'Civil War in Ireland', pp 57–72.

12   Michael Kennedy and Deirdre MacMahon (eds), *Reconstructing Ireland's Past: A History of the Irish Manuscripts Commission* (Dublin, 2010), pp 70–73, plates 28A–C.

13   See for example Canny, 'What really happened in Ireland in 1641', pp 25–42; Raymond Gillespie, 'The end of an era: Ulster and the outbreak of the 1641 rising' in Ciarán Brady & Raymond Gillespie (eds), *Natives and newcomers: essays on the making of Irish colonial society, 1534–1641* (Dublin 1986), pp 191–214; idem, 'Destabilizing Ulster, 1641–1642' in Brian Mac Cuarta (ed.), *Ulster 1641: aspects of the rising* (Belfast, 1993), pp 107–21; Hilary Simms, 'Violence in county Armagh, 1641' in Mac Cuarta (ed.), *Ulster 1641*, pp 123–38; Brendan Scott, 'Reporting the 1641 rising in Cavan and Leitrim' in Brendan Scott (ed.), *Culture and society in early modern Breifne/Cavan* (Dublin, 2009), pp 200–14.

14   As well as the online edition of the depositions, the Irish Manuscripts Commission will publish a print edition of the Ulster depositions. Some of the first research to be undertaken by scholars with access to the full online edition of the depositions can be found in Eamon Darcy, Annaleigh Margey and Elaine Murphy (eds), *The 1641 Depositions and the Irish Rebellion* (London, 2012).

15   Deposition of Owen Connallie, 22 Oct. 1641, MS 809, ff 13r–14v; Andrew Robinson, 'Owen Connolly, Hugh Og MacMachon and the 1641 Rebellion in Clogher' in Darcy, Margey and Murphy (eds), *The 1641 Depositions and the Irish Rebellion*, pp 7–20.

16   For the outbreak of the 1641 rising see Aidan Clarke, 'The genesis of the Ulster rising' in Peter Roebuck (ed.), *Plantation to Partition* (Belfast, 1981), pp 29–45; Michael Perceval-Maxwell, *The outbreak of the Irish Rebellion of 1641* (Montreal, 1994); Canny, *Making Ireland British*; Michael Perceval-Maxwell, 'The Ulster rising of 1641, and the depositions' in *Irish Historical Studies*, 21 (1978), pp 144–67; Canny, 'What really happened in Ireland in 1641?', pp 24–42.

17   Most of these depositions taken in the immediate aftermath of the outbreak of the rebellion can be found in MS 809, ff 5r–104v; deposition of Hugh McMahon, 22 March 1642, MS 840, ff 5r–6v;

18   Information of Hughe oge McMayonn, 23 Oct. 1641, MS 809, ff 15r–v.

19   Information of Lord Mcguire, 26 June 1642, MS 809, ff 24r–5v.

20   Examination of William Moore, 3 Nov. 1641, MS 809, ff 79r–80v; examination of Tirlagh mc Scholane, 3 Nov. 1641, ibid., ff 85r–8v; examination of Edmond O Doghertie, 1 Nov. 1641, ibid., ff 42r–v.

21   Gillespie, 'Destabilizing Ulster', p. 110.

22   Deposition of Stephen Allen, 7 Jan. 1642, MS 832, f. 174r; deposition of Alice Champyn, 14 Apr. 1642, MS 835, ff 196r–7v; deposition of Robert Aldrich, 10 Feb. 1644, MS 834, f. 196v.

23   'The relation of the siedge of the Castle of Lymrick', 1641–2 (BL, Sloane MS 1008, ff 123r–v); Kenneth Wiggins, *Anatomy of a siege: King John's Castle, Limerick, 1642* (Bray, 2000), pp 67–70.

24   First depositions commission, 23 December 1641, MS 812, f. 1r.

25   Second depositions commission, 18 January 1641, ibid., ff 1v–2r; third depositions commission, 11 June 1642, ibid., ff 3r–v.

26   For the justification of the establishment of the depositions commission, see Aidan Clarke, 'The commission for the despoiled subject, 1641–7' in Brian Mac Cuarta

(ed.), *Reshaping Ireland 1500–1700: colonization and its consequences* (Dublin, 2011), pp 241–60 at pp 241–2; HMC, *Ormond*, new series, ii, 67.

27   Clarke, 'The commission for the despoiled subject', p. 260.

28   Depositions taken by the Dublin based commissioners, between 1641 and 1647, are categorised as 'Dublin Originals' on the depositions website.

29   Approximately 55% of the copies made by Waring survive; in some instances only the copy survived. Copies made by Waring are categorised as 'Waring Copies' on the depositions website: Clarke, 'The commission for the despoiled subject', pp 256–7, 259.

30   These depositions are categorised as Bysse depositions: Clarke, 'The commission for the despoiled subject', p. 249.

31   These depositions are categorised as Commonwealth depositions: Clarke, 'The commission for the despoiled subject', pp 241–60.

32   The Bysse depositions for Munster follow a format in which almost every deponent is described as a British Protestant.

33   Deposition of Charity Chappell, 2 July 1642, MS 836, f. 44v; deposition of Ellenor Fullerton, 16 Sept. 1642, ibid., f. 50v.

34   Leinster – 11 volumes (3,786 folios); Munster – 10 volumes (3,241 folios); Connacht – 2 volumes (575 folios).

35   Deposition of Paul Kingston, 22 Sept. 1642, MS 834, ff 30r–v.

36   Deposition of Jane Beere, 4 June 1653, MS 838, f. 98r;

37   Deposition of Margaret Kelly, 24 June 1654, MS 834, f. 44r.

38   Compiled from MSS 832–9.

39   Clarke, 'The commission for the despoiled subject', p. 259.

40   Deposition of Edwards Sanders, 3 May and 9 June 1653, MS 837, ff 59r–60v, 173r–4v.

41   See for example deposition of Richard Magee, 22 Apr. 1653, MS 838, ff 156r–7v; deposition of John O'Sheale, 21 Apr. 1653, ibid., ff 151r–2v; Bryan Magee, 27 May 1653, MS 838, ff 200r–1v.

42   Deponents whose depositions were copied by Waring or who gave multiple depositions are only counted once.

43   Deposition of Sir Phelim O'Neill, 23 Feb. 1653, MS 836, ff 167r–70v; deposition of Donatus Conner, 28 Oct. 1642, MS 818, f. 112r.

44   Deposition of William Hoe, 8 Jan. 1642, MS 833, ff 11r–v.

45   Deposition of Richard Newberrie, 27 June 1643, MS 836, f. 61r; deposition of Peter Gates, 6 June 1643, MS 839, f. 107v.

46   Deposition of Joane Constable, 6 June 1643, MS 836, ff 87r–90v.

47   Deposition of Christopher Meanes, 29 Mar. 1642, MS 833, f. 176r.

48   Deposition of Ambrose Bedell, 26 Oct. 1642, MS 833, f. 105v.

49   Deposition of John Abram, 19 Apr. 1653, MS 837, f. 154r.

50   Deposition of John Kershaw, 8 Jan. 1642, MS 835, f. 124r.

51   Deposition of Jennett Service, 28 Feb. 1653, MS 838, f. 46r.

52   Deposition of Avis Braishawe, 4 Jan. 1642, MS 835, f. 81r.

53   Deposition of Anne Bull, 23 Apr. 1653, MS 834, f. 196r; deposition of Jane Armstronge, 3 May 1653, MS 839, f. 56v.

54   Deposition of Robert Merryman, 25 Apr., 7 and 18 May 1653, MS 837, ff 80r, 132r, 134r.

55   Deposition of Anthony Stratford, 9 Mar. 1644, MS 836, f. 116r.

56   Deposition of Ellen Adams, 23 Aug. 1647, MS 835, f. 257r.

57   Deposition of Philip Taylor, 8 Feb. 1642, MS 836, f. 7r

58   Deposition of Anne Dutton, 2 Nov. 1642, MS 839, f. 129v.

59   Deposition of Alice, countess dowager of Antrim, 9 Feb. 1653, MS 838, ff 22r–3v.

60   Deposition of Anne Bullinbrooke, 22 Dec. 1642, MS 839, f. 30r.

61   Deposition of Jennett Service, 28 Feb. 1653, MS 838, f. 46r.

62   The *OED* defines spinster as 1: A woman (or, rarely, a man) who spins, *esp.* one who practises spinning as a regular occupation; 2: Appended to names of women, originally in order to denote their occupation, but subsequently (from the seventeenth century) as the proper legal designation of one still unmarried.

63   Deposition of Jane Cuthbertson, 3 Feb. 1644, MS 833, f. 243r; deposition of Elizabeth Northope, 3 Feb. 1642, MS 834, f. 136r.

64   Deposition of Katherin Greame, 15 Mar. 1653, MS 838, f. 17r; deposition of Joice Kinde, 10 Feb. 1653, MS 836, f. 143r.

65   Deposition of Gilbert Pemberton, 1 Mar. 1642, MS 836, f. 8r; deposition of George Burne, 12 Jan. 1644, MS 839, f. 39v.

66   Deposition of Anne Dawson, 26 Apr. 1653, MS 836, f. 228r.

67   Deposition of Alice Gregg, 21 July 1643, MS 836, f. 96r; Nicci MacLeod, '"Rogues, Villaines & Base Trulls": Constructing the "Other" in the 1641 Depositions' in Darcy, Margey and Murphy (eds), *The 1641 Depositions and the Irish Rebellion,* pp 113–28.

68   Deposition of Marmaduke Batemanson, 13 Apr. 1643, MS 833, f. 80r.

69   N. Canny, 'The 1641 depositions as a source for the writing of a social history: County Cork as a case study' in P. O'Flanagan and C. Buttimer (eds), *Cork History and Society: interdisciplinary approaches to the history of an Irish county* (Dublin, 1993), pp 249–308 at p. 250.

70   For the development of plantation towns and the 1641 rebellion, see Annaleigh Margey, '1641 and the Ulster Plantation Towns' in Darcy, Margey and Murphy (eds), *The 1641 Depositions and the Irish rebellion,* pp 79–96.

71   William Smyth, *Mapmaking, Landscapes and Memory: a geography of colonial and early modern Ireland,* c. *1530–1790* (Cork, 2006), p. 142.

72   Examination of Elizabeth Gormally, 3 May 1653, MS 838, f. 235r; information of John MacAdam, 14 June 1644, ibid., f. 16r.

73   A sovereign is the mayor of a town, a commonly used term in Ireland. Examination of Thomas Theaker, 18 July 1644, ibid., ff 7r–8v; deposition of John Parry, 30 May 1642, MS 836, f. 65r.

74   Examination of Ardel Mc Mahon, 1 Nov. 1641, MS 809, f. 44r; deposition of Nicholas Simpson, 6 Apr. 1643, MS 834, f. 182r; deposition of George Creighton, 15 Apr. 1643, MS 833, f. 235v.

75   Deposition of John Gowrly, 8 Nov. 1642, MS 836, f. 57r;

76   Deposition of William Smith, 7 July 1642, MS 833, f. 189r.

77   Deposition of Richard Morse, 31 Dec. 1641, MS 835, f. 143v; deposition of Martha Stacke, 8 Jan. 1642, ibid., f. 168r.

78   Deposition of Henry Smith, 11 June 1642, MS 837, f. 14r.

79   Deposition of Arthur Magneiss, 9 June 1642, ibid., f. 9r.

80   Deposition of John Elcock, 7 Jan. 1642, MS 836, f. 4r; deposition of Richard Warrin, 7 Jan 1642, ibid., f. 9r.

81   Clarke, 'The 1641 depositions', p. 119.

82   Ibid., p. 112.

83   Deposition of Henry Smith, 11 June 1642, MS 837, f. 14r; deposition of John Anthony, 28 Feb. 1642, MS 812, f. 34r; deposition of George Casson, 13 July 1642, MS 818, f. 106r; deposition of Edmund Welsh, 22 Jan. 1642, MS 814, f. 118r.

84   John Morrill, 'The rebellion in text and context' in Darcy, Margey and Murphy (eds), *The 1641 depositions and the Irish rebellion,* p. 195.

Deconstructing the reputation of Sir John Clotworthy, 1st Viscount Massereene

'Not otherwise worthy to be named, but as a firebrand brought from Ireland to inflame this Kingdom'.

Andrew Robinson

The reputation of the 'New English' settlers in Ireland in the early modern period has been savaged by both their contemporaries and modern historians. An entrenched persecution *mentalité* remains a potent element of early modern Irish historiographical discourse, and this is particularly true when considering Protestant interlopers and *nouveau riche* that settled in Ireland during the early decades of the seventeenth century. This is reinforced by a general paucity of private letters and correspondence, resulting in a social and political class that retains much of its ill-founded notoriety. Notable exceptions include arrivistes such as Richard Boyle, 1st earl of Cork[1] and Roger Boyle, Baron Broghill and 1st earl of Orrery.[2] Fortunately for historians the Boyles left a substantial archive of diaries, estate records and correspondence which have attracted some scholarly attention. A great deal less is known about other New English settlers such as Sir Charles Coote, 1st Viscount Mountrath, or Roger Jones, 1st Viscount Ranelagh, and even less about the gentry such as Sir William Parsons, Sir Robert Meredith, Hardress Waller or William Jephson.[3] The basis of this chapter therefore is to attempt to go some way towards rectifying this *lacuna* by reconsidering the reputation of Sir John Clotworthy, 1st Viscount Massereene, a key actor in all three Stuart kingdoms in the middle of the seventeenth century.

Sir John Clotworthy's father Sir Hugh, an Elizabethan soldier from Devon, served in Ulster during the Nine Years' War under Sir Arthur

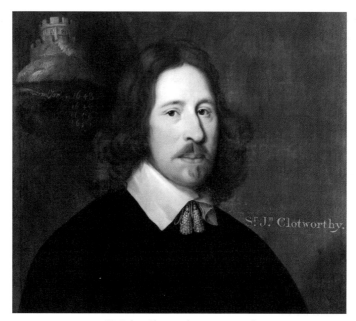

Sir John Clotworthy, courtesy of
Clotworthy House, Antrim Borough Council

Chichester, later lord deputy of Ireland. He and his family played a leading role in fostering Protestant non-conformity from their base of influence in Antrim town during the Six Mile Water religious revival of the mid-1620s, and alongside other planters such as Sir Robert McClelland, controlled large estates owned by the London livery companies. However, Sir John Clotworthy's reputation is largely founded on his activities during the Stuart Civil Wars and Restoration. He proved a key link between the English opponents of Charles I, including the earl of Warwick, Viscount Saye & Sele, Lords Brooke and Robartes, Nathaniel Fiennes and John Pym, and the Scottish Covenanters before and during the Bishops' Wars. As a member of the English Long Parliament he managed the Irish articles of impeachment against Sir Thomas Wentworth during his trial for treason that led to his execution. Clotworthy has also been labelled as a leading member of the 'Presbyterian Party' that sought accommodation with the king as the English Civil War rumbled interminably forward during the 1640s.

Charged with embezzlement of parliamentary money and supplies for Protestant forces in Ireland, accused of obstructing Viscount Lisle in his command of parliamentary forces in Munster, and of conspiring with the royalist lord lieutenant of Ireland James, marquess of Ormond, to surrender Dublin to the royalists, he was himself impeached in 1647 as one of the 'Eleven Members', and then removed from sitting at Westminster as part of Pride's Purge in December 1648. Clotworthy remained imprisoned in various English gaols until November 1651, largely detached from the Irish and British political theatres for several years. However his close association with leading Scots settlers and nonconformists in eastern Ulster meant that Lord Broghill sought Clotworthy's counsel on his appointment as Lord President of the Council in Scotland on the split between Remonstrant and Resolutioner in the Scottish Kirk. Clotworthy later re-entered the political arena once again on the fall of the Protectorate and played a leading part alongside Sir Charles Coote and Broghill in the 1660 Irish Convention that paved the way for the Restoration of Charles II. He also helped to draw up the Act of Indemnity and Oblivion which confirmed the estates of Cromwellian soldiers and adventurers and excluded Irish Catholic 'rebels'.[4]

Like his contemporaries, particularly Coote and Broghill, the slandering of his name by Irish Catholic apologists, royalists, and Westminster Independents has pervaded the historical discourse to such an extent that Clotworthy appears little better than a puritan parody, a religious lunatic driven by sectarian hatred and anti-Catholic bloodlust. Perhaps Clotworthy's most famous description appeared in the second volume of John Nalson's *Impartial Collections* which alleged that Sir John rose to his feet in the House of Commons and delivered a speech to the effect that the conversion of Irish Catholics 'was only to be effected by the Bible in one hand and the sword in the other'.[5] With this flourish of the pen, Nalson perennially cast Clotworthy as an anti-Catholic bigot, and this has remained his epitaph to the present day. However Nalson's attribution of this violently anti-Catholic remark to Sir John does not appear in any of the parliamentary journals kept by Sir Simonds D'Ewes, John Moore, Framlingham Gawdy, Thomas Peyton, Sir John Holland, William Ogden, Sir Ralph Verney, Geoffrey Palmer, Thomas Wyse, or a handful of other anonymous contemporary diaries.[6]

This is not to say that the sentiment Nalson espouses is not without its merits. There are similarly worded statements from various vested parties in the Irish theatre of the Stuart Civil Wars which indicate a contemporary perception that the effusion of Catholic blood was the centerpiece of New English policy in Ireland. However none can be connected definitively to Sir John Clotworthy. The Confederate Irish claimed he was guilty of 'barbarous and unhumane expressions in that Howse against Catholic religion'.[7] No further information is given by the Confederates, but Clotworthy was indeed responsible for one outburst in the House of Commons in which his anti-popery is proudly displayed. Between 17 and 19 July 1641 Giovanni Giustinian, the Venetian ambassador, complained bitterly to the king about the treatment of one of his personal priests, Cuthbert Clopton *alias* Greene, who had been arrested and imprisoned on orders of the House of Commons. Despite the intercession of the king who ordered his release, Sir Henry Vane, secretary of state, refused to do so until both houses of Parliament assented. The French, Spanish and Florentine ambassadors all protested on the matter alleging a direct attack upon the historical customs and conventions granted to foreign ambassadors. Charles I himself noted that the Venetian ambassador was ignorant of laws imposed by Parliament, and therefore moved that no British or Irish-born priest could serve a foreign ambassador, further suggesting that the priest in question should be allowed to leave England and not return. Clotworthy's novel approach for the deliverance of the kingdom from such a Jesuitical plague was to propose a law whereby all priests were castrated, a process he argued that been used successfully by the Swedes and by Bethlen Gabor, prince of Transylvania in the early part of the seventeenth century. William Jephson, the Munster-based planter, seconded Clotworthy's motion. Though it appears that Clotworthy was perfectly serious with his proposal, Sir Simonds D'Ewes noted that the House broke into laughter as it was put forward and stated that the Commons would do well to move quickly from such a motion lest 'the world talk of us for it', leading to the motion's prompt rejection by the House.[8]

No doubt inspired by such outbursts the Confederates claimed that the reason for their rising to arms was:

> That the English and Scotts combyned and joined in a petition to his Majestie to bee lycenced for to come into Ireland *with the Bible in one hand, the Sword in the other* [my emphasis] for to plant their Puritan Anarchicall Religion amongst vs, otherwise after to distroye vs.[9]

This statement is markedly close to that attributed to Clotworthy by Nalson though in this case it is ascribed to a puritanical and Presbyterian hoard of Scots and English malcontents. In a wide ranging list of grievances of 17 March 1643 presented to the king's commissioners at Trim, County Meath, during negotiations towards a cessation of arms, the Confederate nobility accused New English administrators and planters, namely Clotworthy, Sir Adam Loftus, Sir William Parsons, Arthur Hill, and Sir William St Leger, of forcing them to take up arms due to violent anti-Catholicism and inherent corruption in local and national government that targeted loyal Catholics for persecution on account of their religion.[10] However, it was mainly Parsons rather than Clotworthy who incurred the full wrath of the Confederates. As one of the lords justices, his intransigence in refusing a short-term cessation with the Kilkenny Confederates delayed any accommodation between Charles and his Irish Catholic subjects, and his part in drafting the Irish Council's opinion to the king that there could be no lasting peace with them:

> before the sword or famine have so abated them in numbers as that in reasonable time English colonies might overlap them, and so

perhaps frame the residue into English manners and civil cause of life, by trades, or other good industry, to take comfort in a quiet life, the English do plainly forsee it can never be safe for them to cohabit with them, secure for England to enjoy them, or likely that themselves can ever digest into a good to themselves, or profitable to their King or country.[11]

This has been viewed as a 'statement of policy ... notorious for its candid recommendation of wholesale slaughter', a 'searing vision of peace through destruction', and part of a policy paved with 'cold genocidal intent'.[12] Though the harshness of this policy is undeniable, such statements ignore the fact that this reflected a continuation of one facet of New English political and religious thought since the Tudor regime. The Machiavellian ruminations of Tudor settlers like Richard Beacon and Edmund Spenser asserted that Catholic Ireland was naturally rebellious and needed to be broken down and forced to submit before they could be incorporated into the Protestant colony on the island.[13] This strain of radical Protestant ideology found support in the earl of Cork, Sir Charles Coote, Sir Adam Loftus, Sir William Parsons and Sir John Clotworthy. Their suspicion and fear of aggressive counter-reformation Catholicism was confirmed by the events in Ulster after the outbreak of the 1641 rising, and as such, they found a solution in the warnings of a previous generation of settler.

A more notorious example of Clotworthy's anti-Catholicism was the sacking of Henrietta Maria's Royal Chapel at Somerset House on 30 March 1643.[14] During Charles I's Personal Rule, the queen's Catholicism could be tolerated as she proved an invaluable political ally and an avenue of access to the king. However, pilgrimages through Hyde Park to Tyburn to pray for the souls of Catholic martyrs, the establishment of Gregorio Panzani as a permanent Vatican nuncio in her Court, and the leading role of pro-Habsburg advisors such as successive papal agents George Conn and Count Carlo de Rossetti in her inner circle, only heightened fears of European Catholicism at the heart of the English monarchy.[15] The conversion of key royal courtiers in her circle, including her chamberlain, Walter Montagu, Henry Jermyn, Olive Porter, Lady Newport and the duchess of Buckingham, who in 1635, remarried to Clotworthy's local rival Randal MacDonnell, Viscount Dunluce and future second earl of Antrim, only served to increase public consciousness of the Catholic menace at the heart of the royal family.[16] Anxieties about the growing influence of pro-Spanish Catholic courtiers was heightened by the increasingly ostentatious worship by English Catholics and ambassadors of Catholic states at chapels maintained by the queen. At George Conn's Long Acre House, Mass was alleged to be celebrated eight times a day, and the perception that the king was inactive against the threat was fuelled by the actions his wife who routinely ignored his pleas for moderation, most notably when she invited Lady Newport and other converts to Somerset House on Christmas Day 1637 to receive communion. Her confessor Robert Phillip, a Scottish Catholic who moved in an informal circle of Scottish Catholic peers such as the earls of Nithsdale, Abercorn and Winton, created suspicions amongst the Scots Covenanters that there was a Catholic plot to suppress their Presbyterianism.[17]

Public disturbances outside the Royal Chapel at Somerset House had been commonplace occurrences as early as 30 November 1640 when worshippers were attacked with stones and various unspecified weapons.[18] Widespread discontent continued after the recall of Parliament and on 10 May 1641 the Commons ordered the lord mayor of London and the justices of the peace of Surrey, Middlesex and Westminster, to prevent English Catholics from attending religious services in the houses of foreign ambassadors, St James's Palace, or Somerset House.[19] The fourth head of the Ten Propositions passed by both houses of Parliament on 24 June 1641 focused on Henrietta Maria herself and a point was made to single out the Capuchin order for dissolution.[20] This was reiterated on 13 August when the Commons sent the MP Sir Philip Stapleton to the Lords with the message that 'this House takes notice, upon the Apprehension of the Father Sovereign of the Convent of Capuchins, that the Capuchins are very dangerous and active in seducing the King's People', and should therefore be dissolved as per the Ten Propositions.[21] Compromise was still possible and throughout August Edward Sackville, 4th earl of Dorset acted as an intermediary between Parliament and Royal Household, eventually persuaded the queen to agree to confine the Capuchins to Somerset House.[22] However, in the wake of the aftermath of the outbreak of the rising in Ulster, the anti-Catholic cacophony reached a crescendo. On 1 November 1641, news of the rising was delivered to Parliament as the earl of Leicester, the Lord Lieutenant, flanked by sixteen ashen-faced privy councillors, appeared at the bar of the House of Commons. The testimony of Owen O'Connally, formerly a servant of the Clotworthys in Antrim Castle, took centre stage.[23] The outbreak of the 1641 rising and O'Connally's testimony was hugely advantageous to the king's opponents as it presented them with an opportunity to wrest power away from Charles and his 'evil counselors' by creating the mechanisms that permitted them to raise armed forces, prevent the continued religious patronage of Henrietta Maria and realign Caroline foreign relations, moving away from an alliance with Spain towards closer relations with the Dutch republic in particular.[24] The Commons attempted to swiftly remove the Capuchin friars resident in Somerset House. In the same session it was also proposed and later accepted that the oaths of allegiance and supremacy should be tendered to all royal servants, thus barring the queen's access to a Catholic priest which she maintained in blatant contravention of her marriage treaty.[25] Aided by the sensational testimony of Thomas Beale alleging priest-led treachery and insurrection amongst English Catholics, the Houses decided by 18 November that the Capuchins' convent should be abolished, and that foreign ambassadors must dismiss any priest born in the Stuart kingdoms.[26]

It took Parliament almost eighteen months to act decisively and finally liquidate the chapel. Throughout 1642 the Marquis de la Ferte-Imbault, the French ambassador, interceded and argued that removing them was contrary to the queen's marriage treaty. He proposed to keep them 'safe prisoners' at Somerset House, with the doors of the chapel locked and further Mass services banned.[27] By the end of August 1642 the Commons grew impatient and rejected the conciliatory offer and moved that the Lords join with them to have the Capuchins removed from the kingdom.[28] In hyperbolic overtones the Commons moved on 2 September that:

> beholding the Hand of God gone out against this Kingdom, in a Civil War, already begun in the Land; and looking higher than to the pernicious Councellors of it, or wicked Instruments employed in it; and laying to Heart the Displeasure of Almighty God for our many crying Sins, among which none doth more provoke the Eyes of his Jealousy, than the Abomination of Idolatry, and false worship.

The lower house therefore moved that the Capuchins be swiftly banished and all idolatrous paraphernalia destroyed rather than risking the 'farther Incensing of the Wrath of God against this Nation, the Poisoning of the Minds and Consciences of his Majesty's Subjects'.[29]

Despite the Commons repeatedly calling for the peers to move to have the Chapel dissolved and the Capuchins banished, the Lords appeared unwilling to act decisively, rightly concerned at the damage that would ensue to Anglo-French relations. The lower chamber grew increasingly impatient and sought to proceed without the Lords' consent, forming a committee on 5 November to consider how the priests could be 'speedily conveyed out of this Kingdom; and how the Convent may be demolished; and all the superstitious Materials, Pictures, or other such Matters, taken down, defaced, and demolished'. Five days later they moved that all idolatrous monuments be removed, and the friars and monks removed from England, and in early December, Catholic inspired artwork was also to be removed and deposed of.[30]

It still took until March 1643 for a decisive and binding outcome from Westminster. On 13 March the Commons ordered that the sheriffs of London and Middlesex and the committee for the militia of London take the Capuchins into custody, with the earl of Warwick providing a ship to transport them out of the kingdom, and the superstitious monuments inside the chapel destroyed. The following day the French ambassador again attempted to intervene but could do little but delay the inevitable.[31] On 18 March, a committee of Sir John Clotworthy, Henry Marten, Sir John Corbett, Denis Bond and John Gurdon were charged with the removal of the Capuchins and demolishing 'superstitious monuments' there.[32] Despite further last minute interventions of the French ambassador, the committee went ahead with their plans to dissolve the Chapel, and charged that all 'Vestments and Utensils, belonging to the Altars and Chapel of Somerset-house' be burnt, monuments destroyed, and any goods belonging to the French king to be delivered back to him'. They further stated that 'The State shall draw upon themselves the Guilt of Idolatry, by unnecessary permitting, and voluntary conniving at, the Exercise of the Mass within this Realm', further informing the French ambassador that they knew nothing of the queen's marriage treaty, and even if one existed, it was invalid as it was made without the consent of Parliament.[33]

The actions of the committee itself have cast Clotworthy and his cohorts in the worst possible light. Inside the building, it is alleged that Clotworthy smashed the cross and crucifix on the altar. Standing atop it he spotted what he perceived as an excessively decadent painting of the Crucifixion by Sir Peter Paul Rubens and called for a halberd before he:

> struck Christ's face in contempt with such offensive words it would be shocking to repeat them. His second blow was at the Virgin's face, with more hateful blasphemies, and then, thrusting the hook of his halberd under the feet of the Crucified Christ, he ripped the painting to pieces.[34]

A more explicit version is given by Richard O'Ferrall and Robert O'Connell, authors of the *Commentarius Rinuccinianus*, an account of the mission of Giovanni Baptist Rinuccini, appointed Nuncio Extraordinary to the Confederation of Kilkenny by Pope Innocent X in March 1645. They noted that Clotworthy pierced the side of Christ on the crucifix with a lance and mockingly stated 'Let me see if there is even one drop of blood in this worthless wretch'. He then decapitated the infant Jesus in a statue of Christ and the Virgin Mary and leeringly asked the Holy Virgin 'Do you grieve for the injury to your son?', before he removed her head. Clotworthy then went into the garden where he shot his pistol at what he thought was a Capuchin monk, only to discover it was a statute of St Francis attached to a crucifix. After realising his error, the Antrim planter tied a rope to the beam of the crucifix and pulled it to the ground and smashed it into pieces and 'they all ground it into the dirt to dishonour it, and blasphemed it without end'. Clotworthy, Marten and the trained bands that accompanied them then:

filled the holy water fonts with excrement, and when they had taken
away the ornamental flowers, which they thought were artificial,
and divided them among themselves, they tore apart the sacred
books, and destroyed the altars, they broke to pieces an original
painting that had been exquisitely crafted by Paul Rubens, which
was worth ten thousand Turonian pounds, and burnt the relics on a
fire by the church door.

As a final insult, the next morning the raiding party dressed up in Capuchin
vestments and pelted worshippers, 'who were entering the church unaware
of these monstrous crimes', with excrement from the fonts and 'at the same
time intoned I do not know what ugly chants'.[35]

It was not just Catholics that supposedly suffered Clotworthy's
puritanical ire. To defenders of the high Anglican tradition his part in the
execution of Archbishop Laud was a pox not just on Clotworthy himself,
but on wider 'puritan' society. The accounts of Peter Heylyn, which remain
the prevailing historical voice for Clotworthy's part in the episode,
attempted to demonstrate the martyrdom of Laud against the
perniciousness of his enemies by prescribing a high Anglican and Laudian
historical account of the Church of England where Calvinism and
Presbyterianism were cast as the natural birthing mother of civil unrest and
wars between and within nations. Heylyn's account of Clotworthy's
conduct therefore continues this Laudian grand narrative, casting the
'puritanism' of Clotworthy as excessive and dishonourable. In describing
Laud he stated that 'never did man putt off mortality with a better courage,
nor look upon his bloody and malicious enemies with more Christian
charity'.

Sir John Clotworthy, in comparison, is deemed 'a fire-brand brought
from Ireland by the Earle of Warwicke to increase the combustions in this
kingdome'.[36] According to Heylyn, 'that inhumane Sir John Clotworthy',
saw that the 'rude' and 'uncivill' people who mocked Laud as he made his
way to the scaffold had little effect on the prelate and therefore sought to
trick the condemned Archbishop through a series of religious questions.
Heylyn noted that they were 'malicious nonsense to disturb his
meditations, which all the Divell in Hell were not able'. This was 'the same
purpose as was found in the Scribes and Pharisees in propounding
questions to our Saviour; that is to say, either to intrap him in his answers,
or otherwise, to expose him to some disadvantage with the standers by'.
Clotworthy asked him 'What was the comfortablest saying which a dying
man would have made in his mouth'. Laud gave a meek answer, saying
'*cupio dissolvi et esse cum Christo*', in other words to desire to be dissolved
and to be with Christ. Sir John continued as to 'what the fittest speech a
man could use to express his confidence and assurance?' Laud again

temperately replied that such assurance 'was to be found within, and that no words were able to express it rightly'. The Antrim planter was still unimpressed and continued to harass him and demanded that Laud recite some scripture 'whereupon such assurance might be truly founded'. Exasperated, Laud answered that it was 'the Word of God concerning Christ and His dying for us'. The archbishop then turned his back on his puritan foe and then applied himself to the executioner 'as the gentler and discreeter person'.[37] This account has become canon in terms of both the conduct of Laud and the character of Sir John Clotworthy. Particularly problematic is that no counterpart account exists. John Rushworth notes the exchange in the third part of his *Historical Collections,* but this was not published until 1691, and his account of the exchange bears a high degree of semblance with Heylyn, leaving the obvious suspicion that Rushworth used this source and merely attempted to sanitise it.[38]

Nalson's *Impartial Collection* in which the author claimed Clotworthy stated that the conversion of Irish Catholics 'was only to be effected by the Bible in one hand and the sword in the other' was not as 'impartial' as the name suggests. Nalson sought to openly discredit John Rushworth's *Historical Collections of Private Passages of State,* which began its publication in several volumes from 1659. Nalson's subtitle, 'From the Beginning of the Scotch Rebellion to the Murder of Charles I' left the reader in no doubt as to where his loyalty lay, with the pictorial frontispieces and accompanying polemic poem likewise confirming his unimpeachable devotion to the House of Stuart. The first volume depicted Britannia praying amongst the wreckage of church and state 'in the face of an advancing Janus-faced, cloven-footed predator, part presbyter, part papist, trampling the Bible underfoot'. The second volume showed members of the House of Commons violently quarrelling amongst themselves as the king is tossed overboard from the ship of state in the midst of a tempestuous storm. Throughout both volumes Nalson lambasted Rushworth for attempting to lay the blame for the civil war at the feet of Charles Stuart and sought instead to impugn his malignant opposition, including John Pym, the New Model Army, and various Presbyterian ministers. Nalson was convinced that a chief mission of the Presbyterian ministry was to line their own pockets and to play on 'the fears and hopes of the gullible laity and plant themselves in populous centres of trade where they could reasonably expect to reap the easiest success and greatest financial rewards'.[39] In Nalson's opinion these ministers seduced Parliament with their heretical teachings of personal freedom from royal rule, while preachers whipped the populace into a religious frenzy with the ominous threat of mob violence at their disposal should their demands not be met. Clotworthy was an important member of this political and religious community.

Nalson also trumpets a more sophisticated royalist interpretation of the puritan mindset, in which its outwardly divine-driven appearance sought to purify the English nation by drawing on biblical rhetoric, yet it did little more than mask puritan and sectarian anti-monarchical tendencies and heresies. The quote attributed to Clotworthy calls to mind Nehemiah, cup-bearer to the Persian King Artaxerxes, returning to rebuild Jerusalem's crumbling walls. Achieved after just fifty-two days, Nehemiah oversaw the repopulation of the city,[40] the purification of the Jews by entrenching the Ten Commandments in their moral and legal lexicons,[41] the expulsion of non-Israelites from the Promised Land,[42] and forced Jewish men to divorce their Gentile wives.[43] Of particular relevance to Nalson's allusion to converting Catholic Ireland with the Bible in one hand and the sword in the other is Nehemiah 4:16–18 in which the Israelite workmen on Jerusalem's walls used one hand to work whilst grasping a weapon in the other as a means of protection from those who sought to prevent them from carrying out the instructions of the Lord.[44] Nalson likened them to the king's puritan opponents whose building tool was the Bible held in one hand to construct their Godly nation, and the sword an offensive weapon in the other, an armament of compulsion to silence not just Catholics, but any royalist opponents who disagreed with them politically.

Nalson's imputation of anti-Catholicism and anti-monarchialism found their origin in a discourse of victimhood and forced dispossession voiced by Irish Catholics. Nicholas French, Catholic bishop of Ferns, noted in 1668 that Clotworthy was 'a man famous for plundering Somerset House, murdering the Kings subjects and committing many other treasons and horrid crimes … always accounted as violent against the Irish, as he was known to be seditious, and ill-affected to monarchy'.[45] Colonel Nicholas Plunkett, brother of the 3rd earl of Fingal and ascribed as the likely author of 'A Light to the Blind',[46] bemoaned Charles II putting trust in the members of the old Rump Parliament to decide which of the king's citizens should receive pardons. He wrote that the king himself:

> knew who of his people were culpable and who innocent before he left their destinies to the discretionary judgment of an assembly of men taken out of that nation who had made no scruple to murder his royal father, banish himself and his family, destroy the loyalists, and especially the whole Catholic people of Ireland, for adhering to the king's interest.

He continued by asking:

> Why, then, would he leave their dooms to the will, and pleasure of men, amongst whom some, being Cromwellians, might retain their old grudge unto those faithful persons, and particularly keep their former design of ruining the Catholics of Ireland.

Plunkett noted that the king's initial desire was to grant 'stolen' estates back to Irish Catholic loyalists, but Cromwellian land settlement beneficiaries, namely Roger Boyle, Baron Broghill and later 1st earl of Orrery, along with Sir Charles Coote, later 1st earl of Mountrath, 'got together a meeting of their brethren, the usurpers of the Irish estates', in an effort to stop Catholic restitution. 'This fanatic cabal' then sent Sir John Clotworthy, 'that famous plunderer', to England to spread wildly exaggerated accounts on how dangerous it would be for the English interest in Ireland to have Irish Catholics restored to their lands. Clotworthy and 'his fellow-usurpers' then sought to persuade the king and parliament to 'settle that Cromwellian scum of England in their illegal possessions of Irish lands, rather than do justice to the loyal nobility and gentry by restoring unto them their birth-rights'. In Plunkett's view the Old English consistently demonstrated their loyalty to the Crown whilst Clotworthy, Broghill, Coote, 'and the rest of those little fanatic scabs, demonstrated themselves enemies to the solid English interest, that is, to the crown of England'. He noted the feeling amongst the Old English at being punished for their continued loyalty to the House of Stuart and stated, 'Heavens, can anything in nature be more preposterous than to see king Charles exalting his enemies, and such base enemies, nor was ever king so made a fool of by a few of his subject as this prince!'[47] Nicholas French agreed with such a synthesis, asking in *The bleeding Iphigenia*, 'where I say againe, have these men been in the dark day of your Callamitys, and adversitys? what were they then doeing?'[48] The Irish Catholic and tory bitterness that the king had indemnified his enemies and consigned his friends to oblivion is clearly apparent in these texts.

A succession of eighteenth- and nineteenth-century historians, antiquarians and polemicists likewise sought to vindicate the historical reputation of Irish Catholics from accusations of perpetual treachery by impugning key Protestant settlers. Matthew Carey, who sometimes published under the pseudonym Scriblerus O'Pindar[49] quoted Nalson in *Vindiciae Hibernicae: Or, Ireland Vindicated*, stating that Clotworthy was 'one of the most envenomed enemies of the Roman Catholics'.[50] John Curry, physician and historian, also reproduced Nalson in *An historical and critical review of the civil wars in Ireland*. Curry certainly empathised with notions of forced dispossession given that his grandfather died in at Aughrim fighting for the Jacobite cause, and the family lost their land holdings in the aftermath.[51] Matthew O'Connor, a barrister by trade, also relied upon Nalson's quotation in his *The History of the Irish Catholics from the Settlement in 1691*, published in 1813.[52] Many other prominent historians and antiquaries also cited Nalson, including J.P. Prendergast[53] and W.E.H. Lecky,[54] and Thomas Carte in his hagiography of the life of James Butler, 1st Duke Ormond.[55] Two French antiquarians, Augustus Thébaud and Elias Regnault published more controversial titles that sought to defend Irish Catholics and both quoted Nalson. In particular Thébaud, a Jesuit priest writing in 1873, quoted Nalson and Matthew O'Connor and added that the rising was an effort on their part to establish 'in the convulsed island a sort of order in the name of God and the king!', though he naturally excluded the murder of thousands of Protestant settlers in Ulster from his narrative.[56] Clotworthy's reputation even permeated into the realms of historical fiction, with Nalson quoted in Thomas Moore's *Memoirs of Captain Rock*, published in 1824.[57]

In his preface to *The History of the Warr of Ireland from 1641 to 1653, written by an anonymous officer from Sir John Clotworthy's regiment*, the Jesuit-trained scholar Edmund Hogan lambasted the Protestant inspired historiographical interpretations of Thomas Carlyle and J.A. Froude. Hogan referred to the writing style of the anonymous author as being 'simple, straightforward, soldier-like' which was 'refreshing to those, who are disgusted with the 'bend-sinister, the fell temper, and the fevered 'epileptic' and 'demoniac' style of the Carlyle school of history'. Hogan also described it as an antidote and 'wholesome correction' to the 'blood and iron' writing of Froude. Froude, the 'man of Simancas, the king of the inverted commas, the Oracle of the Pigeon-hole', had just published his *English in Ireland in the Eighteenth Century* between 1872 and 1874, filled with 'base words, and heedless hearsays, and frantic oaths, and lewd lies'. Hogan continued that:

> as this little book is the first contribution to Irish History since Mr. Froude published his 'English in Ireland', the editor has been asked and urged to refute him in this Preface; but he has declined, because, to use a mild phrase which was current in 1641, that gentleman 'has cracked his credit' as a historian.

Naturally Hogan did not take his professed high road and included nearly five pages of negative reviews of Froude's work, as well as adding an appendix to his transcription which reproduced Nalson's quotation, and an accusation levelled at Clotworthy for his part in the execution of a number of insurgent McNaughtens in the Route of Antrim.[58] Colonel Alexander McNaughton had alleged in an investigation during the Restoration that the McNaughtons built and maintained a fort near Ballymoney for communal protection from local Irish 'rebels'. He stated that he had sent a letter that affirmed their continued loyalty to Sir John Clotworthy and Sir Mungo Campbell, commander of the regiment based at Ballymoney. McNaughton accused Clotworthy of intercepting the letter intended for Campbell and though he assured McNaughton of his protection, he later assaulted and plundered their fort, arresting all inside. Due in part to the intervention of Sir Mungo Campbell who demanded an explanation,

Clotworthy sent fifteen captives to Ballymoney and promised to send their goods alongside the remaining eighty prisoners the following morning. However, Clotworthy executed them and then fled to England before he could be questioned on the incident by Robert Monro. When he arrived at Westminster he informed Parliament 'hee had stormed a strong ffort wherein there were many Irish and tooke it by fforce, for wch service hee received 1000l'.[59] Naturally Clotworthy denied such accusations, stating that regiments under his command alongside those of Campbell and Sir George Monro had scouted the area in order to clear it of insurgents, and that his major, Owen O'Connally, his former servant and the individual responsible for first uncovering and reporting the 1641 rising to startled lords justices, took the decision to take the fort.[60] Major O'Connally and 500 men moved against the fort and 'the bloody rebels of the Root', to prevent its continued use as a base to attack Coleraine.

On capturing the fort O'Connally found a set of captured regimental colours belonging to Archibald Stewart's regiment that had sallied from Coleraine on 11 February 1642 only to be routed by the insurgents. Clotworthy stated that all the captives had been brought to Ballymoney where Captain Campbell, a brother of Sir Mungo, kept guard. Captain Campbell separated fifteen men after 'speaking ye Highland Irish wth divers of them, finding as it appears by the sequell some of them such as hee had kindnesse for, or intended to make use of'. Clotworthy then noted that he, Sir Mungo Campbell and Monro conversed privately until they heard several volleys of musket fire and found the rest of the prisoners had been executed. Clotworthy explained that some of the prisoners were MacDonnells with whom the Campbells of Argyll had an ancient feud, and that they 'mett wth that fate which either sept gaue ye other coming vnder their power, for such hath beene their constant practice as is notoriously knowne'.

There is a certain hypocrisy in contemporaneous and more modern castigation of Clotworthy in failing to control his soldiers in this instance given the many accounts of barbarity perpetrated in the early months of the 1641 rising by the levies under Sir Phelim O'Neill or Rory O'More, condemned even by Owen Roe O'Neill when he arrived in Ireland in July 1642. Clotworthy himself argued that it was a case of revenge for the soldiers killed coming out of Coleraine in search of food on 11 February. He pointed out that finding the English colours in the fort would have brought them to a trial of Court Martial 'where they could not have escaped'.[61]

The accounts of Carey, O'Connor, Curry, Froude and others are clearly a product of their contemporary environments and reflect the degrees to which the 1641 rising and the subsequent Cromwellian reconquest of Ireland continued to form a key element of the historical identities of both

Irish Protestants and Catholics. Carey, O'Connor and particularly Curry's publications make significant contributions that shed light on the social and cultural *milieu* of educated Catholics outside of the sinews of high-political activism from which they were barred. Their work represents an Irish Catholic interpretation of the rising that sought to downplay Protestant allegations of atrocity and premeditated massacre, and argued that the continuation of the annual state celebrations of 23 October and entrenchment of massacre in the Protestant *mentalité* was little more than an overt ploy to justify disenfranchising Catholics and maintaining a Protestant elite. In attacking this quintessential exemplar of Catholic treachery in Ireland, they attempted to create a discourse and vehicle through which they could regain full economic, political and social rights that had been denied them through the imposition of the Penal Laws.

This is especially true after passage of the 1800 Act of Union and the ever increasing demands for Catholic Emancipation. As the Home Rule crises loomed on the horizon, the histories of Froude, Lecky and Prendergast demonstrate the deep division that existed between Protestant and Catholic over the proposed devolution. Materials from the 1641 depositions and from Sir John Temple's *The Irish rebellion: or the history of the beginning and first progress of the general rebellion raised within the kingdom of Ireland, upon the three and twentieth day of October, 1641* reappeared in print during the third Home Rule Crisis (1912–14), and during the War of Independence, (1919–21). The events of 1641, 1689 and 1798 reinforced Catholic treachery in many Protestant and Unionist eyes and in spite of the scholarly efforts of Prendergast, Robert Dunlop, Cardinal Moran, J.T. Gilbert and Thomas Fitzpatrick, the narrative produced by Froude, Mary Hickson and Ernest Hamilton amongst others reaffirmed this mindset. Unionists instead drew inspiration from the 1643 Solemn League and Covenant in the creation of the 1912 Ulster Covenant, both instruments that united Protestants in England, Scotland and Ireland against the threat posed by covert popery.[62]

Among the Irish Catholics the rapaciousness of the English Protestant planter in Ireland, like Sir John Clotworthy, retained its potency in the early part of the twentieth century as Home Rule reappeared on the political horizon. To the Home Rule MP Timothy Healy, the trickery and skullduggery of Edward Carson and James Craig easily found historical parallels in key English *arrivistes* of the seventeenth century. A narrative of forced dispossession, lies and deceit is captured in his *Stolen Waters: A Page in the Conquest of Ulster,* a legalistic *tour de force* that decried the moral standing of settlers in Ulster, particularly Sir John Clotworthy and Sir Arthur Chichester, lord deputy of Ireland.[63]

One biographer of Healy highlighted the deep personal sense of injustice and dispossession which informed his writing. The Healys once possessed ancestral lands in east Muskerry, but following the forfeiture of lands held by the Jacobite earl of Clancarty in the aftermath of the Williamite War and imposition of the Penal Laws, they lost most of their estate. Healy's grandfather bitterly regaled him with tales of deposition at the hands of a turncoat relative who converted to Protestantism in order to obtain their property, which left the young Healy with 'an abiding fixation with dispossession'.[64] The Nationalist MP reacted bitterly to the 1911 decision of the House of Lords regarding fishing rights on Lough Neagh and the River Bann when the court ruled that they continued to be vested in the descendants of the Chichesters despite Oliver Cromwell having restored the charter to the Bann and Lough Neagh to the London companies on 24 March 1657. Healy asked 'why the welfare of the fishermen of five counties should count as naught against the parchments of bygone rascaldom?' He noted that the fisheries of the River Bann were 'the pearl of the adventure', but Chichester 'robbed them [the Londoners] of their bargain and annexed the river for himself'.

According to Healy, 'the Plantation methods of the City were merciful to the Irish when contrasted with the ruthlessness of individual planters'. This apparent leniency led to a great deal of dissatisfaction on the part of many Ulster undertakers who instead sought to 'make the native his prey', whilst Crown officials in Dublin and their 'local cronies in Ulster' were active enemies of the Londoners. Clotworthy, an 'acolyte' of Chichester, gained himself rent of Lough Neagh for 99 years on 13 May 1656, but also the lease on the Bann through skullduggery on 14 August of the same year, confirmed by Charles II on 15 November 1660. Healy, like Plunkett before him, lamented that Charles had not stood firmly against the outright dishonesty of the planters and Cromwellian adventurers, of whom 'crime dogged every step of each of the Patentees in their disloyal enterprise'. Healy continued that:

> the misconduct of the Chichesters, Clotworthys, and others seems impossible to those who would judge the men of the seventeenth century by the standards of to-day. The history of that time, however, shows that acts of turpitude in State affairs were an everyday business.

Healy postulated a historical trajectory of English misrule in Ireland, connecting the 1911 *debâcle* in the House of Lords with the oppression of Chichester, Sir John Davies and others in the early Jacobean period, concluding that 'so the freebooter who robbed the Earls of Ulster, three hundred years ago, again triumphed in the award which enables his descendants to doom to destruction a remnant of the people he hated'.[65]

Conversely, Presbyterian historians and antiquarians largely saw

Clotworthy in a very different light and sought to rescue his reputation from nationalist slurs, painting him as a Godly stalwart, a religious hero and spiritual leader rather than a rapacious land speculator. Patrick Adair, one of the most important chroniclers of early Presbyterian history in Ulster commended Sir John, his father Sir Hugh and their respective wives as being key supporters of the early Presbyterian Church amongst a sea of religious degenerates, hosting conventicles and helping it to spread in Antrim. He referred to them as 'the honourable family in Antrim' whose example 'instantly other gentlemen followed … of whom the Gospel made a clear and cleanly conquest'. Adair described Sir John's wife and mother as 'very religious and virtuous women', with his elderly mother is particular viewed as a 'noble and religious matron'.[66] However, such claims must be approached with caution given that Adair penned his history in the halcyon days of the Restoration. Many other non-conformist ministers such as Robert Blair and John Livingstone presented their religious loyalty as being unimpeachable and their bond with the Crown unbreakable, thereby aiming to reach an accommodation with the Restoration administration.[67] Nonetheless, later Presbyterian chroniclers relied on Adair in accounting for the spread of Presbyterianism in eastern Ulster in the early seventeenth century.

Thomas McCrie, a mid-nineteenth century Free Church of Scotland minister and antiquarian, extolled Clotworthy as 'one of nature's noblemen, one of the few whose names, when the bigotry of that period has been written, will be found honourable exceptions to the degeneracy of the age'.[68] James Seaton Reid, a nineteenth-century minister and historian who charted the history of the Presbyterian Church in Ulster, expressed extreme skepticism about John Nalson's oft-restated quotation dismissing it as little more than royalist slander and 'totally at variance with the whole tenor of his character and actions'. Reid instead praised the Clotworthy family for their patronage of Presbyterianism in County Antrim, and in particular for their support of the Six Mile Water religious revival in the east of the province in the mid-1620s.[69]

One dissenting Presbyterian voice that is heavily critical of Clotworthy is that of Rev. George Hill, minister, historian, antiquarian and poet. His studious collection of materials on the Montgomerys of eastern Ulster, the MacDonnells of Antrim and the Plantation of Ulster remain important sources for historians.[70] Hill dubbed Clotworthy, a 'zealous Presbyterian', referring to him as 'one of the most successful of the many selfish aliens who first plundered and afterwards would have gladly extirpated the native Irish inhabitants'. He lambasted Clotworthy who 'although not as cunning, perhaps as Coote or Boyle [Broghill], was quite as selfishly opposed to the just claims of his Catholic countrymen'. Instead of praising Cromwellian Adventurers as pious members of a Godly society that stood against the murderous bloodlust of Irish Catholics, he painted them as disloyal and traitors to the Stuart Crown; who waged war on Charles I and held his son to ransom on the eve of the Restoration, tricking their way to titles, confiscated land, and wealth. Hill relied on Nicholas French's interpretation of the 1662 Act of Settlement and the eleven qualifications drawn up by Clotworthy and his cohorts to prevent Irish Catholics from receiving pardons and restoration of their land, 'that monstrous issue', 'flagrant misrepresentation', and 'master-piece' of Protestant chicanery ensured that the Adventurers kept their ill-gotten settlements'. The author also sought to restore the reputation of the leaders of the 1641 rising, portraying it as the two-tiered 'rebellion', an interpretation which is now widely accepted by historians. He noted that instead the:

> oppressions of Chichester, Falkland and Wentworth in hunting for defective titles among the Catholics, by the insolence and rapacity of such men as Parsons, Clotworthy, Broghill, Coote, St Leger, and a swarm of the same class, had laid the foundations of revolt wide and deep.[71]

This analysis is initially puzzling given his training as a Presbyterian minister. One possible explanation is his own religious bias as a remonstrant minister, serving in Ballymoney in 1834 and Crumlin in 1837 in the aftermath of the bitter internal struggles of the Synod of Ulster which culminated in withdrawal of 'New Light' and Arian inspired ministers to form the Remonstrant Synod in 1830. In contrast James Seaton Reid, who praised the Clotworthys, served as moderator of the synod of Ulster in 1827 at the very height of the controversy and played a leading role in the union with the Secession Synod to form the General Assembly of the Presbyterian Church in Ireland in 1840. Andrew Holmes explains this as part of a wider process of the shaping and reshaping of Ulster Presbyterian identity between the failed 1798 rebellion and the third Home Rule Bill crisis in 1914.

Whereas Reid and his subscribing contemporaries increasingly made reference to the Scottish providence of the Presbyterian Church in Ulster, Hill utterly rejected this link between the Scottishness of Ulster and the improvement of the province, theological orthodoxy and religious and civil liberties. Hill saw the roots of sectarian strife in Ireland in the mid-seventeenth century, the Williamite war and the 1798 rebellion as seeded in the plantation of Ulster and abhorred the cruelty and rapaciousness of English and Scottish planters towards Irish Catholics.[72] Indeed he likened his own personal struggles with the Synod of Ulster to the reciprocal political support between Clotworthy, Broghill and the resolutioners against the remonstrants in Ulster and Scotland in the 1650s, thus transferring his own religious frustrations and bias into the past.[73]

Running almost parallel to this strain of Presbyterian historical consideration of the past, various Anglican historians and antiquarians attempted to restore the reputation of the martyred Archbishop Laud. Given the prevailing influences of the Oxford Movement and Tractarianism obvious contemporary parallels could be draw from the liturgical and ceremonial innovations brought by Laud in the seventeenth century. John Parker Lawson, a high church Scottish episcopal minister who later supported the Oxford Movement and Tractarianism[74] praised Laud while describing Clotworthy as a 'furious enthusiast, one of those revolutionary demagogues'.[75] Charles Webb Le Bas, a fellow of Trinity College Cambridge, prebendary of Lincoln Cathedral, and principal of the East India College, Haileybury, noted that Clotworthy, who 'had already distinguished himself by his outrageous violence against the earl of Strafford', was a 'coarse fanatic' who harassed Laud on the scaffold with 'impertinent and insidious questions'.[76] Le Bas was associated with a group of high Anglicans known as the 'Hackney Phalanx',[77] and used his various publications to establish theological links between Caroline divines and the Oxford Movement of 1833.[78]

Frederick Faber, fellow of Balliol College Oxford, a high Anglican with Tractarian sympathies who later converted to the Roman Catholic Church in 1845,[79] decried Clotworthy as a 'violent and wrong-headed man, an enthusiast, and very furious as a demagogue'.[80] The seven-volume publication *The works of the Most Reverend Father in God, William Laud, D.D. sometime lord archbishop of Canterbury* by William Scott and James Bliss remains a vital source for the early modern historian, but has often been treated as a primary source rather than a biased account which also happens to include personal letters and correspondence. William Scott, who produced two of the seven volumes for the Library of Anglo-Catholic Theology, identified with the martyred Anglican prelate. As curate of Christ Church, Hoxton, London, he attempted to apply Tractarian principles to worship by reordering the liturgy and ceremonial structure of the church, and was accused of placing candles on the altar, crossing himself, robing the choir in surplices, and partaking in other practices seen as ritualistic in 1840s' England. While leading a service in St Andrew's, Well Street, London, on 30 November 1850, he was threatened by an anti-ritualistic mob due to his innovation.[81] The author's sympathy for Laud resonates across their seven volumes, and Peter Heylyn's account of Laud's execution is reproduced verbatim.[82] Heylyn excoriates Sir John Clotworthy as 'a fire-brand brought from Ireland by the Earle of Warwicke to increase the combustions in this kingdome'.[83] Other nineteenth-century contemporaries described him as a 'noisy, hard-hearted puritan'[84] and 'puritanical bigot',[85] thus reinforcing his puritan reputation that has been further entrenched by twentieth-century historians such as Hugh Trevor-Roper[86] and Charles Carlton.[87]

Paul Klemp's study of the execution of Laud portrays it as a symbolic 'theatre' performance, with the scaffold the 'stage' on which the judicial killing of the prelate took place. This is extremely persuasive given Laud's attempts to control how he would be represented to the crowd and in posterity, with his speeches and prayers transcribed and later printed.[88] Heylyn's account can be read as being a major part in this performance, intending to preserve Laud's stoic and Christ-like conduct *immemorium*, and add another martyr alongside the likes of Thomas Cramner, Hugh Latimer and Nicholas Ridley to reinforce a pantheon of religious virtue against a puritanical horde that later also executed the king. As such, it is highly noticeable that Laud's death signified his vision for the Anglican Church as a whole, full of ritualism and symbology.[89] Heylyn noted that Laud was mocked by members of the crowd, bringing immediate comparisons to the treatment of Jesus by his Roman guards as he walked to the cross.[90] He also asked his executor to remove those underneath the scaffold lest they be covered in his blood, and to prevent them from creating 'relics' from his clothes and blood, recalling the soldiers who cast lots to see who would get Jesus' clothes.[91] Sir John Clotworthy took an unwitting role in this symbolic performance, with Heylyn comparing his taunting of Laud to the sponge and vinegar offered to Jesus on the cross.[92] Heylyn also stated that just after Laud's beheading the sun disappeared behind the clouds and the city was covered in darkness for several hours, a direct parallel to the death of Jesus where the darkness reigned from noon to three in the afternoon.[93] Klemp states that Clotworthy's part in challenging this cacophony of symbology was to deliberately break with the *ars moriendi* tradition, the act of preparing a man to die well.[94]

It is questionable whether Clotworthy's intervention was merely just a vindictive personal attack or a religiously inspired tirade by the Antrim planter; rather his questions attempted to undermine the heavily ritualistic performance of the prelate. Nothing could be more dangerous to the parliamentary war effort in 1645 than to have the blood of a 'godly' martyr on their hands, potentially offering explicit evidence of their extremism in religious outlook as well as in political and constitutional thought. Certainly Heylyn's *Cyprianus Anglicus,* published in 1668 during the Restoration acted as a retrospective rebuke to those who had murdered Laud and Charles I in bouts of religious separatism and in this account Clotworthy unwittingly reinforced royalist and high Anglican perceptions of their religious and military foes. 'Thus Laud fell, and the Church fell with him'.[95] Sir John Clotworthy shed few tears for the archbishop's popishly inspired Church as he exited Laud's carefully staged martyrdom finale.

It is evident that Sir John Clotworthy's reputation is, like that of many other historical figures, a hodge-podge of legend, myth, innuendo and fact. No historian can be insulated from the influence of contemporary politics and ideology, but this chapter should suggest a corrective to those historians who believe that a 'scientific' approach to history is 'boring' and urge instead a return to the polemical histories written by the likes Eoin MacNeill and Edmund Curtis.[96] The interpretation of the character of Sir John Clotworthy that has pervaded historical discourse reflects the dangers of uncritically accepting the evidence of contemporary commentators like Peter Heylyn and John Nalson, whose 'histories' are based as much in polemic as in fact. Where archival material and correspondence of the New English settler community does not exist, historians must be more inventive, more searching and be more analytically rigorous when dealing with the sources that are in their possession. Only then can the study of the maligned Protestant settler in early modern Ireland move beyond the narrow strictures of ideological and political interpretation.

I would like to thank William P. Kelly, Éamonn Ó Ciardha, Patrick Little and Robert Armstrong for their insightful comments on various drafts of this chapter. I also gratefully acknowledge the funding provided by the Northern Ireland Department of Education and Learning (DEL) which made this research possible.

Notes

1   P. Little, 'The Geraldine ambitions of the first earl of Cork' in *Irish Historical Studies*, 33 (2002), pp 151–68; C. Tait, 'Colonising memory: manipulations of death, burial and commemoration in the career of Richard Boyle, first earl of Cork (1566–1643)' in *Proceedings of the Royal Irish Academy*, section 101C (2001), pp 107–34; P. Little, 'The earl of Cork and the fall of the earl of Strafford, 1638–41' in *Historical Journal*, 39 (1996), pp 619–35; N. Canny, *The upstart earl: a study of the social and mental world of Richard Boyle, first earl of Cork, 1566–1643* (Cambridge, 1982); T.O. Ranger, 'Richard Boyle and the making of an Irish fortune, 1588–1614' in *Irish Historical Studies*, 10 (1956), pp 257–97; idem, 'The career of Richard Boyle, 1st earl of Cork, in Ireland, 1588–1643' (unpublished D.Phil. thesis, University of Oxford, 1959).

2   P. Little, *Lord Broghill and the Cromwellian union with Ireland and Scotland* (Woodbridge, 2004); idem, 'An Irish Governor of Scotland: Lord Broghill, 1655–1656' in A. Mackillop & S. Murdoch (eds), *Military governors and imperial frontiers c. 1600–1800* (Leiden, 2003) pp 79–97; J. Kerrigan, 'Orrery's Ireland and the British problem, 1641–1679', in D.J. Baker & W. Maley (eds), *British identities and English renaissance literature* (Cambridge, 2002), pp 197–225.

3   In the case of Irish-based MPs of the Long Parliament, such as Waller, Jephson and others including Arthur Jones and Sir Robert King, the painstaking research of the History of Parliament Trust, to be published in 2016, will yield much further information. Jane Ohlmeyer's weighty and fresh look at the Irish aristocracy in *Making Ireland English: The Irish Aristocracy in the Seventeenth Century* (New Haven & London), offers an alternative view of the noble classes based on cross-

confessional deference and honour. It is certainly suggestive, but not wholly convincing given the almost entirely confessional nature of both Protestant 'British' and Covenanting armies, and the Confederates throughout the 1640s and 1650s. Obvious exceptions such as Sir Charles Coote's support of Catholic officers Thomas and Dudley Costello are merely exceptions to the rule, but important in contextualising the nature of the war in Ireland. For further consideration of cross confessional links across the Stuart kingdoms see the persuasive argument of Patrick Little in '"Blood and Friendship": The Earl of Essex's Protection of the Earl of Clanricarde's Interests, 1641–6' in *English Historical Review*, 112 (1997), pp 927–41; Micheál Ó Siochrú has also highlighted the possibility of both forced and voluntary recruitment of native Catholics into Cromwell's New Model Army: M. Ó Siochrú, *God's Executioner: Oliver Cromwell and the Conquest of Ireland* (London, 2008), pp 205–11.

4   For Clotworthy's career during the Stuart Civil Wars see A. Robinson, '"Not otherwise worthy to be named, but as a firebrand brought from Ireland to inflame this Kingdom": The political and cultural milieu of Sir John Clotworthy during the Stuart Civil Wars' (unpublished Ph.D. thesis, University of Ulster, 2012).

5   J. Nalson, *An Impartial Collection of the Great Affairs of State* (1683) II, p. 536.

6   Most of these sources have been transcribed and published. The most extensive is M. Jansson (ed.), *Proceedings in the opening session of the Long Parliament: House of Commons* (7 vols Suffolk, 2000–2007). These cover the period November 1640–September 1641 and include the diaries of D'Ewes, Moore, Gawdy, Peyton, Holland, Wyse, Palmer, Holles, Lord Robartes, and several anonymous entries. The diaries of D'Ewes have been reproduced elsewhere such as W. Notestein (ed.), *The journal of Sir Simonds D'Ewes from the beginning of the Long Parliament to the opening of the trial of the earl of Strafford* (New Haven, 1923); W.H. Coates (ed.), *The journal of Sir Simonds D'Ewes from the first recess of the Long Parliament to the withdrawal of King Charles from London* (New Haven, 1942); W. H. Coates, A.S. Young & V.F. Snow (eds), *The private journals of the Long Parliament, 3 January to 5 March 1642* (New Haven, 1982); W.H. Coates, A.S. Young & V.F. Snow (eds), *The private journals of the Long Parliament, 7 March to 1 June 1642* (New Haven, 1987); W.H. Coates, A.S. Young & V.F. Snow (eds), *The private journals of the Long Parliament, 2 June to 17 September 1642* (New Haven, 1992); See also For example M. Jansson (ed.), *Two diaries of the Long Parliament* (Gloucester, 1984); A.H.A. Hamilton, *Note book of Sir John Northcote* (London, 1877); J. Bruce (ed.), *Notes of proceedings in the Long Parliament ... by Sir Ralph Verney, Knight*, (London, 1845). For the problems with using these sources see J. Morrill, 'Reconstructing the history of early Stuart parliaments' in *Archives*, 21 (1994), pp 67–72; idem, 'Paying one's D'Ewes' in *Parliamentary History*, 14 (1995), pp179–86; idem, 'Getting over D'Ewes' in *Parliamentary History*, 15 (1996), pp 221–30. For an alternative and a reply to Morrill, see M. Jansson, 'Dues paid' in *Parliamentary History*, 15 (1996), pp 215–20.

7   J.T. Gilbert (ed.), *History of the Irish confederation and the war in Ireland. With correspondence and documents of the Confederation and of the administrators of the English government in Ireland. Contemporary personal statements, memoirs, etc.,* ii (1882), pp 226–42 [A Remonstrance of Grievances in the behalf of the Catholics of Ireland, delivered by the Lord Viscount Gormanston, Sir Lucas Dillon, Knight, Sir Richard Talbot, Baronet, and John Walsh, Esquire, thereunto authorized by the Confederate Catholics of Ireland, to his Majestie's Commissioners, at the town of Trim, in the county of Meath, on the 17th of March, 1642, to be presented to his most excellent Majestie].

8   *CSPV, 1640–1642*, pp 189–93; *LJ*, IV, pp 317–318; *CJ*, II, p. 216; BL, Harleian
     163, f. 407r; Bod. Lib., Rawlinson MS. D. 1099, f. 146v in Jansson, *Proceedings
     in the Opening Session*, V, p. 686; University of Minnesota Library, MS 137,
     p. 144 in Jansson, *Proceedings in the Opening Session*, VI, p. 9.
9   TCD, MS 840, f. 25r.
10   Gilbert, *History of the Irish Confederation* (1882) I, pp 226–42.
11   *HMC Ormond*, II, pp 244–53 [lords justices and Council to Charles I, 16 March
     1643].
12   W.P. Kelly, 'The Early Career of James Butler, Twelfth Earl and First Duke of
     Ormond, 1610–43' (unpublished Ph.D. thesis, Cambridge University, 1995),
     pp 376–78. For details of the rivalry between Parsons and Ormond, see chapters
     six and seven; R. Armstrong, *Protestant war: the 'British' of Ireland and the wars of
     the three kingdoms* (Manchester, 2005), pp 82–3; P. Lenihan, *Consolidating
     conquest: Ireland 1603–1727* (Harlow, 2008), p. 111; M. Ó Siochrú, *Confederate
     Ireland, 1642–1649: A Constitutional and Political Analysis* (Dublin, 1999), pp 62–4.
13   For further reading see N. Canny, *Making Ireland British, 1580–1650* (Oxford,
     2001), pp 1–58, esp. pp 42–58; A. Hadfield & W. Maley (eds), E. Spenser, *A
     View of the Present State of Ireland from the first printed edition* (1633) (Oxford,
     1997), pp 22–26, 48, 143–45, 151–53; P. Palmer, *Language and conquest in early
     modern Ireland: English Renaissance Literature and Elizabethan Imperial Expansion*
     (Cambridge, 2001); V. Carey, 'The Irish face of Machiavelli: Richard Beacon's
     Solon his folie and republican ideology in the conquest of Ireland' in H. Morgan
     (ed.), *Political Ideology in Ireland, 1541–1641* (Dublin, 1999), pp 83–109; N.
     Canny, 'Poetry as politic: a view of the present state of *The Faerie Queene*' in
     Morgan (ed.), *Political Ideology in Ireland*, pp 110–26; E. Flanagan, 'The anatomy
     of Jacobean Ireland: Captain Barnaby Rich, Sir John Davies and the failure of
     reform, 1609–1622' in Morgan (ed.), *Political Ideology in Ireland*, pp 158–80; B.
     Bradshaw, 'Sword, Word and Strategy in the Reformation in Ireland' in *Historical
     Journal*, 21 (1978), pp 475–502.
14   S.R. Gardiner, *History of the great civil war, 1642–1649* (London, 1893) I, p. 118.
15   R.M. Smuts, 'The Puritan followers of Henrietta Maria in the 1630s' in *English
     Historical Review*, 93 (1978), pp 26–45; idem, 'Religion, European Politics and
     Henrietta Maria's Circle, 1625–41', in E. Griffey (ed.), *Henrietta Maria: Piety,
     Politics and Patronage* (Aldershot, 2008), pp 13–38; M.A. White, *Henrietta Maria
     and the English Civil Wars* (Aldershot, 2006), pp 21–5, 31–2.
16   Montagu had converted to Catholicism in 1635 after travelling from the English
     embassy in Paris to Loudun to witness the exorcisms of several Ursuline nuns. He
     had been secretly ordained abroad in 1637 and was appointed chamberlain to the
     queen at Somerset House and was prominent in his conviction that she must
     actively and more aggressively propagate the Catholic religion in England, and
     campaigned for the establishment of the papal agency at her Court. Jermyn
     converted in 1636. George Conn converted Olive Porter, niece of the duke of
     Buckingham and the wife of Charles's pro-Spanish bedchamber servant Endymion
     Porter. She converted her father, Lord Boteler, and her brother-in-law, Captain
     Tom Porter, on their deathbeds in 1637. She further attempted the same with the
     marchioness of Hamilton though ultimately failing due to the intense efforts of
     the marchioness' father, the earl of Denbigh, and the bishop of Carlisle. She was
     more successful with the duchess of Buckingham, widow of 1st duke, then
     married to the earl of Antrim. The most high profile of the converts was Lady
     Newport, wife of Mountjoy Blount, 1st earl of Newport, half-brother to the earls
     of Holland and Warwick. Newport himself was a staunch Protestant and sought

William Laud's assistance to punish Montagu and Sir Toby Matthew who he believed was to blame for his wife's conversion. See White, *Henrietta Maria*, pp 31–3; S. Poynting, '"In the Name of all the Sisters": Henrietta Maria's notorious whores' in C. McManus (ed.), *Women and Court Culture at the Courts of the Stuart Queens* (Basingstoke, 2003), pp 163–85; C. Hibbard, *Charles I and the Popish Plot* (Chapel Hill, 1983), p. 55; R.G. Asch, 'Porter, Endymion (1587–1649)', *ODNB*, http://www.oxforddnb.com/view/article/22562; J. Ohlmeyer, 'MacDonnell, Katherine, duchess of Buckingham and marchioness of Antrim (1603?–1649)', *ODNB*, http://www.oxforddnb.com/view/article/69581.

17   D. Freist, 'Popery in perfection? The experience of Catholicism: Henrietta Maria between private practice and public discourse' in M.J. Braddick & D.L. Smith (eds), *The Experience of Revolution in Stuart Britain and Ireland – Essays for John Morrill* (Cambridge, 2011), pp 42–5; White, *Henrietta Maria*, pp 34–5.

18   *CSPV, 1640–1642*, pp 96–7.

19   *CJ*, II, p. 141; *CSPV, 1640–1642*, pp 148–9.

20   *CJ*, II, pp 184–5; *LJ*, V, pp 285–7.

21   *CJ*, II, pp 255, 256.

22   *CJ*, II, pp 252–3; *LJ*, IV, pp 364, 367; See also D.L. Smith, '"More Posed and Wise Advice": The Fourth Earl of Dorset and the English Civil Wars' in *Historical Journal*, 34 (1991), pp 805–06; for Dorset's relationship with Henrietta Maria more generally, see D.L. Smith, 'Catholic, Anglican or Puritan? Edward Sackville, Fourth Earl of Dorset and the Ambiguities of Religion in Early Stuart England' in *Transactions of the Royal Historical Society (Sixth Series)* (1992), pp 105–24.

23   *CJ*, II, pp 300–301; Coates, *The Journal of Sir Simonds D'Ewes*, pp 60–65.

24   Instead of focusing on raising money for relief in Ireland and rewarding O'Connally for his service, the House debated the reliability of the earl of Portland, whose father had died a Catholic, as a reliable governor of the Isle of Wight. The House of Lords refused to dismiss him, and the Commons continued to waste the following day on the issue without a resolution. It was also proposed that leading Catholic peers in England be secured, and that any English papists residing in Ireland return within one month for such a proclamation. See M. Perceval-Maxwell, *The Outbreak of the Irish Rebellion of 1641* (Dublin, 1994), pp 276–7; *CJ*, II, pp 30, 300, 365; Coates, *The Journal of Sir Simonds D'Ewes*, pp 62–4, 67–8; *CSPD, 1641–1643*, p. 154; for some aspects of foreign relations with Spain and the United Provinces, see A.J. Loomie, 'Alonso de Cárdenas and the Long Parliament, 1640–1648' in *English Historical Review*, 97 (1982), pp 289–307; S. Groenveld, 'The English civil wars as the cause of the first Anglo-Dutch war, 1640–52' in *Historical Journal*, 30 (1987), pp 541–66.

25   *CJ*, II, pp 300–01, 305; *LJ*, IV, p. 501; *CSPV, 1640–1642*, pp 243–45; Anon., *A True relation of the treaty and ratification of the marriage concluded and agreed upon betweene our soveraigne Lord Charles by the grace of God, king of great Britaine, France and Ireland, and the Lady Henretta Maria daughter of France and sister to His most Christian Majestie the French King* (London, 1642); Freist, 'Popery in perfection?', pp 34–35, 37–42, 45–47.

26   Beale alleged that two priests, Father Andrewes and Father Jones, alongside Lord Herbert, the son of the earl of Worcester, plotted to murder 'that rascally Puritan Pym' and others members of the Lords and Commons; *CJ*, II, p. 320; T. Beale, *A True Discovery of a Bloody Plot Intended to Have Been Put in Practice* (London, 1641); John Davis, Servant, to Mistris Lewis, *A great discovery of a damnable plot at Rvgland castle in Monmoth-shire in Wales related to the high court of Parliament / by Iohn Davis, November the 12, 1641* (London, 1641); Anon., *A discovery of a*

horrible and bloody treason and conspiracie against the Protestants of this kingdome in generall, but especially against divers of the nobility, and many of the honourable House of Commons in Parliament, and also against some of the citizens of London (London, 1641); Anon., *A Damnable Treason by Contagious Plaster of a Plague-Sore* (London, 1641); Anon., *Fourewonderfull, bloudy, and dangerous plots discovered and brought to light by Gods providence with the manner and means of their discoverie and prevention* (London, 1641); Anon., *Englands deliverance, or, a great discovery, being a true relation of the treacherous practices of the papists now resident in this citie* (London, 1641); the Venetian ambassador called these attempts by Parliament an effort to draw support away from the king and 'stir them up by all manner of inventions'; *CSPV, 1640–1642*, pp 250–52; Matthew Carey wrote of Beale that 'of all the informers of those days, a certain Thomas Beale, a taylor, merited a palm. None of confraternity could stand a comparison with him': M. Carey, *Vindiciae Hibernicae: Or, Ireland Vindicated: An Attempt to Develop and Expose a Few of the Multifarious Errors and Falsehoods Respecting Ireland, in the Histories of May, Temple, Whitelock, Borlase, Rushworth, Clarendon, Cox, Carte, Leland, Warner, Macaulay, Hume, and others: particularly in the legendary tales of the pretended conspiracy and massacre of 1641* (2nd ed., Philadelphia, 1823), p. 286; for anti-Catholicism in England more generally, see R. Clifton, 'The popular fear of Catholics during the English Revolution' in *Past & Present*, 52 (1971), pp 23–55; D.A. O'Hara, *English Newsbooks and Irish Rebellion: 1641–1649* (Dublin, 2006), pp 29–32; J. Cope, *England and the 1641 Irish Rebellion* (Woodbridge, 2009), pp 96–7.

27   The Venetian ambassador wrote that his French counterpart was 'afraid that he will be blamed by his sovereign for not having insisted with sufficient vigour on their remaining, in accordance with the articles of the marriage treaty': see *CSPV, 1640–1642*, pp 294–5; *CJ*, II, pp 458, 464; *LJ*, V, p. 335; *CSPV, 1642–1643*, pp 7–8.

28   *CJ*, II, p. 747.

29   Ibid., p. 749.

30   The committee was made up of Sir John Glyn, Sir Peter Wentworth, Sir John Bampfylde, Sir Henry Mildmay, Walter Strickland, Sir Bulstrode Whitelocke, Sir Oliver St John, Sir Edmund Prideaux, Sir John Maynard and Laurence Whitaker: *CJ*, II, p. 835; for the Commons continuing to press the Lords to action, see *CJ*, II, pp 780, 790, 802, 824, 830, 843, 907, 909; *LJ*, V, p. 372; a committee including Sir John Glyn, Sir Oliver St John, Sir Edmund Prideaux, Sir Henry Mildmay, Francis Rous, and Samuel Browne was appointed on 12 December to offer reasons to the Lords for demolishing pictures and monuments at Somerset House and for the removal of the Capuchins: see *CJ*, II, p. 885. The Venetian ambassador noted that the House of Lords refused to allow the Capuchins to be sent away until the queen returned from the United Provinces: *CSPV, 1642–1643*, pp 150–64.

31   *CJ*, II, pp 1001, 1003, 1004; *LJ*, V, pp 679–80, 681, 683, 686. By accident or design an agent of the ambassador delivered his reasons in French which caused continual delays in the upper House whilst they were translated.

32   *CJ*, III, pp 8, 19, 23. Sir Edward Patheriche was added to the committee on 28 March. See *CJ*, III, p. 23.

33   *CJ*, III, pp 24, 25, 27, 36, 46–7, 48, 54; *LJ*, V, pp 687, 692. After the committee for the removal of the Capuchins had acted the Lords demonstrated their ill-ease with its actions, stating that 'the Lords would have taken notice of this, but that it concerned the Publick; but have passed it by, as they conceive

They themselves have been in this Business. As for the removing of the Capuchins from a monastical Way, they did approve of it; and if they had been taken along in this Business, something might have been better done, in the managing of it; but conceive it much in order to the publick Safety, that a neighbour Prince, so potent, might not remain unsatisfied'.

34   'Relation non signée du pillage effectué par les Puritaines à la résidence des Capucinsaumôniers de la reine d'Angleterre à Somerset', Paris, Archives du Ministre des Affaires Etrangères, Correspondence Polique d'Angleterre, Tome 49, ff 279–280 in J. Mauzaize, *la Rôle et l'action des Capucins de la Province de Paris dans la France religieuse du XVIIeme siècle* (Paris, 1978), pp 1,504–08, quoted in A.J. Loomie, 'The Destruction of Rubens's 'Crucifixion' in the Queen's Chapel, Somerset House' in *The Burlington Magazine*, 140 (1998), pp 680–81.

35   *Commentarius Rinnucinianus*, I, ff 607v–08. The Royalist press too reported details of Clotworthy's sojourn with London trained bands to the Queen's Chapel. Peter Heylyn, who recounted Clotworthy's alleged mocking of Archbishop Laud on the scaffold, also noted the sacking of the Queen's Chapel. He described it as being part of a plot to justify Parliament's breach in relations with France. He also noted that Mr Browne, the housekeeper of the chapel, had been called before the Lords to account for his refusal to open its doors when Clotworthy called upon him 'for no other reason, but because he was an honest man, and would not willingly betray the trust reposed in him'. See P. Heylyn, *Mercvrivs Avlicvs, communicating the intelligence and affaires of the court to the rest of the Kingdome* (2–9 April 1643) (Oxford, 1643), pp 172–73; the Venetian ambassador also noted that the soldiers who entered the chapel caused a great amount of damage to the arms of France. See *CSPV, 1642–1643*, p. 264.

36   P. Heylyn, *A Briefe Relation of the Death and Svfferings of the Most Reverend and Renowned Prelate the L. Archbishop of Canterbvry: with, a More Perfect Copy of His Speech, and Other Passages on the Scaffold, Than Hath beene Hitherto Imprinted* (Oxford, 1645), p. 24. This passage was subsequently tempered by its author in *Cyprianus Anglicus* to the better-known 'Not otherwise worthy to be named, but as a firebrand brought from Ireland to inflame this Kingdom'.

37   Peter Heylyn, *Cyprianus Anglicus: or, the History of the Life and Death, of The most Reverend and Renowned Prelate William by Divine Providence, Lord Archbishop of Canterbury, Primate of all England, and Metropolitan, Chancellor of the Universities of Oxon (London, 1668)*, pp 436–7; idem, *A Briefe Relation*, p. 15; idem, *Mercvrivs Avlicvs, communicating the intelligence and affaires of the court to the rest of the Kingdome* (5–12 January 1645) (Oxford, 1645), p. 1,334.

38   [Sir *John Clothworthy*.] What special Text of Scripture is most comfortable now to a Man in his departure?
      [*Cant.*] *Cupio dissolvi & esse cum Christo.*
      [Sir *John Clothworthy*.] That is a good desire, but there must be a Foundation for that desire and assurance,
      [*Cant.*] No Man can express it, it is to be found within.
      [Sir *John Clothworthy*.] It is founded upon a Word though, and that Word would be known.
      [*Cant.*] That Word is the Knowledge of Jesus Christ and that alone.
      See J. Rushworth, *Historical Collections of Private Passages of State*, part III, vol. ii, p. 785.

39   R.C. Richardson, 'Re-fighting the English Revolution: John Nalson (1637–86) and the Frustrations of Late Seventeenth-Century English Historiography' in *European Review of History: Revue europeenne d'histoire*, 14 (2007), pp 1–20; R.C.

Richardson, 'Nalson, John (*bap.* 1637, *d.* 1686)', *ODNB*,
http://www.oxforddnb.com/view/article/19734; as William P. Kelly has
demonstrated, Nalson like other contemporary antiquarians, used the papers of
the duke of Ormond as research tools and even consulted with Butler about some
of the events in which he participated. Such a prescription informed Nalson's
writing, and Ormond's loyalty to the House of Stuart stood in stark comparison
to that of Clotworthy and his New English contemporaries: Kelly, 'The Early
Career of James Butler', pp 3–4.

40   Nehemiah 7: 4–72.

41   Nehemiah 8.

42   Nehemiah 13:1–3.

43   Nehemiah 13: 24–29.

44   Nehemiah 4:16–18, [16] And it came to pass from that time forth, that the half
of my servants wrought in the work, and the other half of them held both the
spears, the shields, and the bows, and the habergeons; and the rulers were behind
all the house of Judah. [17] They which builded on the wall, and they that bare
burdens, with those that laded, every one with one of his hands wrought in the
work, and with the other hand held a weapon. [18] For the builders, every one
had his sword girded by his side, and so builded. And he that sounded the
trumpet was by me.

45   Nicholas French, *A narrative of the settlement and sale of Ireland whereby the just
English adventurer is much prejudiced, the antient proprietor destroyed, and publick
faith violated: to the great discredit of the English church, and government, (if not re-
called and made void) as being against the principles of Christianity, and true
Protestancy / written in a letter by a gentleman in the country to a noble-man at court*
[Lovain, 1668], pp 2–4.

46   For further consideration of Plunkett's manuscript see Ó Siochrú, *Confederate
Ireland 1642–1649*, pp 269–71; P. Kelly, '"A light to the blind": the voice of the
dispossessed elite in the generation after the defeat at Limerick' in *Irish Historical
Studies*, 24 (1985), pp 431–62.

47   J.T. Gilbert (ed.), *A Jacobite narrative of the war in Ireland, 1688–1691* (Dublin,
1892), pp 2–7, 15–17.

48   N. French, *The bleeding Iphigenia or An excellent preface of a work unfinished,
published by the authors frind, with the reasons of publishing it* (Louvain, 1674),
pp 46–47.

49   W. Clarkin, *Mathew Carey: a bibliography of his publications, 1785–1824* (New
York, 1984); E.C. Carter II, 'The political activities of Mathew Carey, nationalist,
1760–1814' (unpublished Ph.D. thesis, Bryn Mawr College, 1962).

50   M. Carey, *Vindiciae Hibernicae*, pp 318, 359. In a twist of fate, Carey had earlier
published a woodcut on 5 April 1784 in which he depicted a spoof hanging of
John Foster, chancellor of the exchequer, which led to his arraignment before the
House of Commons alongside his brother, and eventual imprisonment in
Newgate Prison. Upon his release he fled to America on 7 September 1784 to
escape a libel action, dressed as a woman. This seems someone ironic in the
circumstances considering Sir John Clotworthy himself is reported to have a
penchant for hiding himself as a disfigured woman as he travelled from Ulster,
through Scotland to Westminster during January 1643. In a further twist, John
Foster, later Baron Oriel, had one surviving son, Thomas Henry, who married
Lady Harriet Skeffington, *suo jure* Viscountess Massereene, in 1810. This tied the
Foster and Clotworthy-Skeffington families, and the current Viscount is named
John David Clotworthy Whyte-Melville Foster Skeffington, 14th Viscount

Massereene and 7th Viscount Ferrard. That Carey lampooned Foster and subsequently attacked the historical reputation of Sir John Clotworthy, 1st Viscount Massereene, seems purely coincidental: J. Archbold & S. Kleinman, 'Carey, Mathew', *DIB*, http://dib.cambridge.org/viewReadPage.do?articleId=a1474; A.P.W. Malcomson, 'Foster, John Baron Oriel', *DIB*, http://dib.cambridge.org/viewReadPage.do?articleId=a3339#; W. Ingler, *Certaine informations from severall parts of the kingdome , 30 Jan–6 Feb 1643* (London, 1643), p. 18; Armstrong, *Protestant War*, p. 90, fn. 111.

51   J. Curry, *An historical and critical review of the civil wars in Ireland: from the reign of Queen Elizabeth, to the settlement under King William. Extracted from Parliamentary records, state acts, and other authentic materials* (Dublin, 1810), pp 148, 618; for further examination of Curry and O'Connor, see J. Gibney, 'Walter Love's "Bloody Massacre": an unfinished study in Irish cultural history, 1641–1963' in *Proceedings of the Royal Irish Academy*, 110C (2010), pp 217–37; idem, '"Facts newly stated": John Curry, the 1641 Rebellion, and Catholic Revisionism in Eighteenth-Century Ireland, 1747–80' in *Eire-Ireland*, 44 (2009), pp 248–77.

52   O'Connor based his publication on manuscript materials belonging to his grandfather Charles O'Connor, a founder of the Catholic Association in Dublin in 1756 alongside Curry and Thomas Wyse to campaign for legal recognition of the property rights of Irish Catholics. See Matthew O'Conor, *The History of the Irish Catholics from the Settlement in 1691 with a View of the State of Ireland from the Invasion by Henry II. to the Revolution* (Dublin, 1813), p. 31; D. Ó Catháin, 'Charles O'Conor of Belanagare: antiquary and Irish scholar' in *Journal of the Royal Society of Antiquaries of Ireland*, 119 (1989), pp 136–63; D. Ó Catháin, 'O'Conor, Charles', *DIB*, http://dib.cambridge.org/viewReadPage.do?articleId=a6652#; D. Murphy, 'O'Conor, Matthew', *DIB*, http://dib.cambridge.org/viewReadPage.do?articleId=a6657.

53   J.P. Prendergast, *The Cromwellian settlement of Ireland?* (2nd ed., London, 1870), p. 78

54   W.E.H. Lecky, *A history of Ireland in the eighteenth century* (London, 1892) I, p. 40.

55   T. Carte, *A general history of England from the earliest times*, IV (London, 1755), p. 382; T. Carte, *The life of James, Duke of Ormond: containing an account of the most remarkable affairs of his time, and particularly of Ireland under his government; with appendix and a collection of letters, serving to verify the most material facts in the said history* (Oxford, 1851) II, pp 235–36.

56   Augustus Thébaud, *The Irish Race in the Past and in the Present* (New York, 1873), p. 266; Elias Regnault, *The Criminal History of the English Government: From the First Massacre of the Irish, to the Poisoning of the Chinese* (Philadelphia, 1843), p. 22.

57   T. Moore, *Memoirs of Captain Rock: the celebrated Irish chieftain, with some account of his ancestors* (London, 1824), pp 67–8.

58   E. Hogan (ed.), *The History of the Warr of Ireland from 1641 to 1653: By a British Officer of the Regiment of Sir John Clotworthy* (Dublin, 1873), pp 154–5; J.H. Ohlmeyer, *Civil War and Restoration in the Three Stuart Kingdoms: The career of Randal MacDonnell, marquis of Antrim, 1609–1683* (Cambridge, 1993), pp 112–13.

59 TNA, S.P. 63/307/2. Both this account and that given by Clotworthy put the number of those killed at around eighty, not 100 as Jane Ohlmeyer claims: Ohlmeyer, *Civil War and Restoration*, p. 113.

60 See A. Robinson, 'Owen Connolly, Hugh Óg MacMahon and the 1641 Rising in Clogher' in E. Darcy, A. Margey & E. Murphy (eds), *The 1641 Depositions and the Irish Rebellion* (London, 2012), pp 7–20.

61 TNA S.P. 63/307/2. This seems a perfectly plausible explanation given the risible conditions experienced by those subjects besieged inside the walls of Coleraine in early 1642. Sir James MacDonnell, Turlough Oge O'Cahan and Alasdair MacColla, kinsman to the earl of Antrim, betrayed Archibald Stewart who had previously aided Antrim in defending his estates and tenants in the initial outbreak of the rising. They attacked and massacred between sixty and eighty soldiers guarding the river crossing at Portnaw, County Antrim, before attacking Ballintoy Castle, Oldstone Castle, capturing Ballycastle, and burning Dunluce town to the ground. At first MacDonnell demanded that Coleraine be surrendered by Archibald Stewart, which Stewart refused, and the town was besieged, and on 11 February, Stewart and around 600 men and a troop of horse sallied from the town in search of much needed supplies, only to be ambushed at Laney, near Ballymoney. Stewart's forces were routed on this 'blacke ffriday', losing several hundred men after a devastating Highland charge. As a result, conditions within the walls of the town became ever worse for Protestant refugees. Anthony Stephens, a solider in the regiment of Sir John Borlase, one of the lords deputies, claimed that he saw 140 corpses lying in an uncovered pit 'layd soe thick & closse together as he may well compare it to the makeing or packing vp of herrings', and estimated that since the outbreak of the rising some 7,000–8,000 British Protestants had died through disease and starvation. He claimed that that conditions were so bad that some were forced to 'eate & feed vpon their owne children & others & those that could gett the flesh of dogs Catts horses raw hides ratts or such Like': see Hogan, *The History of the Warr*, pp 22–3; D. Stevenson, *Scottish Covenanters and Irish Confederates* (Belfast, 1981), pp 100–02; J.R. Roberts, *Clan, king, and covenant: history of the Highland clans from the Civil War to the Glencoe Massacre* (Edinburgh, 2000), p. 39; idem, 'The Desertion of the Irish by Coll Keitach's Sons, 1642' in *Irish Historical Studies*, 21 (1978), pp 76–77; Ohlmeyer, *Civil War and Restoration*, pp 106–09; for contemporary accounts see examination of Neileoge ô Quin, 17 March 1653, TCD MS 838, ff 39r–39v; examination of James Gray, 28 February 1653, TCD MS 838, f. 46v; examination of Jennett Service, 28 February 1653, TCD MS 838, ff 46r–46v; examination of Fergus Fullerton, 1 March 1653, TCD MS 838, ff 56r–56v; examination of Robert ffuthy, 2 March 1653, TCD MS 838, ff 59r–60r; examination of Donnell crone McCart, 15/3/1653, TCD MS 838, ff 78r–78v; examination of John Blaire, 8 March 1653, TCD MS 838, ff 68v–69v; deposition of Robert Waringe, 12 August 1642, TCD MS 839, ff 110r–v; examination of George McLaughlin, 3 March 1653, TCD MS 838, ff 61v–62r; examination of Donnoghy ô Cahan, 8 March 1653, TCD MS 838, ff 70v–71r; deposition of Anthony Stephens, 25 June 1646, TCD MS 830, ff 41r–43v.

62 R. Dunlop, 'The depositions relating to the Irish massacres of 1641' in *English Historical Review*, 1 (1886), pp 740–44; M. Hickson, *Ireland in the seventeenth century or the Irish massacres of 1641–2: their causes and results* (2 vols, London, 1884); T. Fitzpatrick, *The Bloody Bridge and other papers relating to the insurrection of 1641* (Dublin, 1903); Lord E.W. Hamilton, *The Irish rebellion of 1641, with a history of the events which led up to and succeeded it* (London, 1920). For analysis

for the historical debate and its importance during the Home Rule crises see C. Brady, 'Offering offence: James Anthony Froude (1818–94), moral obligation, and the uses of Irish history' in V. Carey & U. Lotz-Heumann (eds), *Taking Sides? Colonial and Confessional Mentalites in Early Modern Ireland: Essays in honour of Karl S. Bottigheimer* (Dublin, 2003), pp 266–90; N. Vance, 'The problems of Unionist literature: Macaulay, Froude and Lawless' in D.G. Boyce & A. O'Day (eds), *Defenders of the Union: A Survey of British and Irish Unionism since 1801* (London, 2001), pp 176–87; D. McCartney, 'James Anthony Froude and Ireland: an historiographical controversy of the nineteenth century' in *Irish University Review*, 1 (1971), pp 238–57.

63   T.M. Healy, *Stolen Waters: A Page in the Conquest of Ulster* (London, 1913).

64   F. Callahan, *T.M. Healy* (Cork, 1996), pp 4–6.

65   Healy, *Stolen Waters*, pp 2–3, 246–59, 295–309, 313–26, 328–52, 380–81, 399.

66   P. Adair, *A True Narrative of the rise and progress of the Presbyterian Church in Ireland from 1623 to 1670* (Belfast, 1866), W.D. Killen (ed.), pp 16–17, 83–4, 206, 319.

67   R. Armstrong, 'Ireland's Puritan Revolution? The Emergence of Ulster Presbyterianism Reconsidered' in *English Historical Review*, 121 (2006), pp 1,048–57; J. McCafferty, *The reconstruction of the Church of Ireland: Bishop Bramhall and the Laudian reforms, 1633–1641* (Cambridge, 2007), pp 177–92; idem, 'When reformations collide' in A.I. Macinness & J.H. Ohlmeyer (eds), *The Stuart Kingdoms in the Seventeenth Century* (Dublin, 2002), pp 186–203.

68   T. McCrie (ed.), *The Life of Mr. Robert Blair, containing his autobiography from 1593 to 1636* (Edinburgh, 1848), p. 71; W.A.J. Archbold, 'McCrie, Thomas (1797–1875)', Rev. Lionel Alexander Ritchie, *ODNB*, http://www.oxforddnb.com/view/article/17407.

69   J.S. Reid, *History of the Presbyterian church in Ireland* (Belfast, 1867) I, W.D. Killen (ed.), pp 108–09, 299, fn. 6.

70   G. Hill (ed.), *The Montgomery manuscripts; 1603–1706 / compiled from family papers by W. Montgomery* (Belfast, 1869); idem, *An historical account of the MacDonnells of Antrim: including notices of some other septs, Irish and Scottish* (Belfast, 1873); idem, *An historical account of the plantation of Ulster at the Commencement of the Seventeenth Century, 1608–1620* (Belfast, 1877).

71   Hill, *An historical account of the MacDonnells of Antrim*, pp 59 fn. 36, 290–91, 294 fn. 91, 317 fn. 176, 327 fn. 189; Nicholas French, *A narrative of the Earl of Clarendon's settlement and sale of Ireland whereby the just English adventurer is much prejudiced, the antient proprietor destroyed, and publick faith violated: to the great discredit of the English church, and government, (if not re-called and made void) as being against the principles of Christianity, and true Protestancy, written in a letter by a gentleman in the country to a noble-man at court* [Louvain, 1668], pp 83–5.

72   See for example several articles by Holmes that reinforce this point: A.R. Holmes, 'Covenanter politics: evangelicalism, political liberalism and Ulster Presbyterians, 1798 to 1914' in *English Historical Review*, 125 (2010), pp 340–69; idem, 'Presbyterian religion, historiography, and Ulster Scots identity, c. 1800 to 1914' in *Historical Journal*, 52 (2009), pp 615–40; idem, 'Irish Presbyterian commemorations of their Scottish past, c. 1830–1914' in F. Ferguson & J.R.R. McConnel (eds), *Ireland and Scotland in the nineteenth century* (Dublin, 2009), pp 48–61.

73   I would like to thank Andrew Holmes for a discussion on this point. For background on Broghill, see Patrick Little, *Lord Broghill and the Cromwellian*

union with Ireland and Scotland (Woodbridge, 2004); Stevenson, *Scottish Covenanters,* pp 290–91.

74   R. Strong, 'Lawson, John Parker (*d.* 1852)', *ODNB,* http://www.oxforddnb.com/view/article/16206.

75   J. Lawson, *The Life and Times of William Laud, D.D., Lord Archbishop of Canterbury* (London, 1829), pp 506–07.

76   C.W. le Bas, *The Life of Archbishop Laud* (London, 1836), pp 324–5.

77   This group of Anglican high-churchmen, led by Joshua Watson and his brother-in-law Henry Handley Norris, sought to defend the position of the Church of England against any concessions granted to Catholics and Dissenters. They rejected the doctrine of salvation by grace through faith alone, instead favouring grace transmitted through baptism with final justification conditional on the holiness of one's life and good works. The Anglican Church was viewed as the successor to the ancient Catholic Church by preserving historic ordination procedure and liturgy, but without the corruptions of the Roman Church. For further reading see M. Smith, 'Hackney Phalanx (*act.* 1800–1830)', *ODNB,* http://www.oxforddnb.com/view/theme/52465; C.B. Faught, *The Oxford Movement: a thematic history of the Tractarians and their times* (Pittsburgh, 2004); P.B. Nockles, *The Oxford Movement in context: Anglican high churchmanship* (Cambridge, 1994); A.B. Webster, *Joshua Watson: the story of a layman, 1771–1855* (London, 1954).

78   J.H. Overton, 'Le Bas, Charles Webb (1779–1861)', *rev.,* M.C. Curthoys, *ODNB,* http://www.oxforddnb.com/view/article/16253.

79   S. Gilley, 'Faber, Frederick William (1814–1863)', *ODNB,* http://www.oxforddnb.com/view/article/9050.

80   F.W. Faber, *The autobiography of Dr. William Laud, Archbishop of Canterbury, and Martyr, collected from his remains* (Oxford, 1839), p. 432.

81   G. Le G. Norgate, 'Scott, William (1813–1872)', *rev.* N.W. James, *ODNB,* http://www.oxforddnb.com/view/article/24937.

82   W. Scott & J. Bliss (eds), *The works of the Most Reverend Father in God, William Laud, D.D. sometime lord archbishop of Canterbury* (Oxford, 1854) IV, pp 438–9.

83   P. Heylyn, *A Briefe Relation of the Death and Svfferings of the Most Reverend and Renowned Prelate the L. Archbishop of Canterbvry: with, a More Perfect Copy of His Speech, and Other Passages on the Scaffold, Than Hath beene Hitherto Imprinted* (Oxford, 1645), p. 24.

84   J.N. Norton, *Life of Archbishop Laud* (Boston, 1864), pp 249–50.

85   G.L. Craik, *The pictorial history of England: being a history of the people, as well as a history of the kingdom* (London, 1840) III, p. 326.

86   H. Trevor-Roper, *Archbishop Laud, 1573–1645* (2nd ed., London, 1965), p. 428.

87   C. Carlton, *Archbishop William Laud* (London, 1987), p. 226.

88   P.J. Klemp, '"He that now speakes, shall speak no more for ever": Archbishop William Laud in the theatre of execution' in *Review of English Studies,* new series, 61 (2010), pp 188–213.

89   Ibid., pp 194–6, 208–09, 210–12.

90   Heylyn, *A Briefe Relation,* p. 23; Matthew 27:29–31; Mark 15:17–20: Luke 22:63–5, 23:37–9; John 19:1–3.

91   Heylyn, *A Briefe Relation,* p. 23; Matthew 27:35; Mark 15:24; Luke 23:34; John 19:23–24.

92   Heylyn, *A Briefe Relation,* p. 24; Matthew 27:34; Mark 15:36; Luke 23:36; John 19:28–29.

93 Heylyn, *A Briefe Relation,* p. 26 noted that 'the Sunne shone on him as he prayed on the blocke and then disappeared after beheading'; Matthew 27:45; Mark 15:33: Luke 23:44–45.
94 Klemp, '"He that now speakes"', pp 205–07.
95 Peter Heylyn, *Cyprianus Anglicus,* p. 539.
96 S.G. Ellis, 'Nationalist Historiography and the English and Gaelic Worlds in the Late Middle Ages' in *Irish Historical Studies,* 25 (1986), pp 1–18; B. Bradshaw, 'Nationalism and Historical Scholarship in Modern Ireland' in *Irish Historical Studies,* 26 (1989), pp 329–51; S.G. Ellis, 'Historiographical Debate: Representations of the Past in Ireland: Whose Past and Whose Present' in *Irish Historical Studies,* 27 (1991), pp 289–308; B. Bradshaw & T. Graham, 'Interview: A Man with a Mission' in *History Ireland,* 1 (1993), pp 52–5.

Index